CA$HVERTISING

How to Use
More Than 100 Secrets
of Ad-Agency Psychology
to Make BIG MONEY
Selling Anything to Anyone

DREW ERIC WHITMAN

CAREER
PRESS

This edition first published in 2009
by Career Press, an imprint of
Red Wheel/Weiser, llc
With offices at:
65 Parker Street, Suite 7
Newburyport, MA 01950
www.careerpress.com
www.redwheelweiser.com

ISBN: 978-1-60163-032-2

Library of Congress Cataloging-in-Publication Data
available upon request.

Edited and typeset by Kara Reynolds
Cover design by The DesignWorks Group

Printed in Canada
MAR

Want Better Results From Your Advertising?
Ad expert Drew Eric Whitman says:

"I'll teach you more about how to create powerfully effective moneymaking advertising than your competitors will know in their entire careers—*guaranteed*!"

Dear Friend:

Did you ever see a magician saw a lady in half? A sword swallower gobble down a 28-inch blade? A swami walk barefoot over a bed of fiery coals?

These tricks are amazing. Mind-boggling. And seemingly impossible. But the truth is, if you knew the secrets behind them, you could do them too.

Creating Effective Advertising Is No Different!

Because, just as do those uncanny magicians, today's advertising experts have special tricks of their own. They use *consumer psychology*, powerful methods that influence people to read their ads, and buy like crazy. In fact, New York's biggest ad agencies use these tactics every day. And it doesn't matter what their clients sell; these tricks work for *every* business. Plus, they're 100 percent legal, ethical, and powerful.

Best of all...

(Go to next page)...

If You're Ready to Learn the Secrets...
I'm Ready to Teach You!

Invest a few tax-deductible* dollars in this fun, fast, and easy-to-read book. In these fast-reading pages, I arm you with techniques that can help make your competition virtually disappear. I teach you how to turn weak, ineffective ads, brochures, sales letters, flyers, e-mails, and Websites into psychologically potent money-makers that help boost your business *fast*. No special skills are required. And most tricks cost nothing to use. Once you know the secrets, it's easy!

Meet you inside!

Drew Eric Whitman

P.S. I *knew* you'd read this P.S. How? Because the P.S. is one of the most important parts of any sales letter, and it's often read first, before the body copy. Always use the P.S. to restate your offer here. Repeat your contact information, and push your prospect to take action! Now, turn the page and start reading!

* Consult your tax advisor.

To my loving parents, Bob and Eileen, for fostering my childhood passion for advertising and business...even when I should have been doing my homework.

To my wonderful wife, Lindsay, for supporting my creative ideas, wacky plans, and off-beat business ventures that often keep me awake until dawn.

To my son, Chase, for helping me realize what's truly most important in life...and to slow down and enjoy it.

To Gary Halbert, the "Prince of Print," for helping me develop my voice when I was a mere copy cub.

To John Caples, who taught me the definition of great advertising.

To Walter Weir, whose dedication and personal instruction helped me land my first agency copywriting job in 1984.

And to all who find value in what I do.

Thank you.

Drew Eric Whitman, July 2008

Contents

CHAPTER 3: AD-AGENCY SECRETS: 41 PROVEN TECHNIQUES FOR SELLING ANYTHING TO ANYONE   79

CHAPTER 4: HOT LISTS: 101 EASY WAYS TO BOOST YOUR AD RESPONSE

* 22 Response Superchargers
* 9 Ways to Convey Value
* 13 Ways to Make Buying Easy
* 11 Ways to Boost Coupon Returns
* 46-Point "Killer Ad" Checklist

Preface

Trash, trash, trash!

That's how I describe 99 percent of today's advertising. It's dumb. Boring. Weak. Not worth the paper it's printed on.

Am I angry? No. Realistic? Yes. But don't just take *my* word for it. Look in your trash can. How much of the nonsense you get in the mail winds up there before you open it? How much of what you *do* open ends up in the same place before you finish reading the first few lines? How many TV commercials have convinced you to buy? How many e-mails have persuaded you to spend money? How many Websites have bored you to tears?

I rest my case.

The Bottom Line: The Goal of Advertising Is to Get People to Act

Whether you want them to ask for more details, shoot you some cash via PayPal, or whip out their Visa, it's *action* that makes advertising pay off. Because advertising is *not* journalism. It's not news reporting. As a journalist, your job is to report what happened. You don't need people to respond to succeed. Your primary interest is that they're accurately informed and somewhat entertained.

When you write *advertising*, on the other hand, you want people to do more than just read. You want them to do more than simply say,

11

"Wow...great ad!" and then toss it into the kitchen trash on top of the grapefruit skins. No. You want people to *act now*, to place an order or request information that's designed to persuade them to order. Let's not kid each other, we advertise for one reason: to make money. Period.

Do you know why most advertising today is so lousy? It's because most people in advertising today don't know a damned thing about what makes people buy. Believe it or not, it's true. They like to be cutesy and clever. They like to win awards for creativity that do nothing more than boost their egos and waste thousands of dollars for their clients. Most advertisers (and their agencies) don't know how to capture people's imagination, and make them *want* to open up their wallets and spend money. When I asked my mentor, advertising great Walter Weir, "Why is most advertising today so lousy—even the ads put out by giant and successful companies?" He replied in his deep, radio announcer-like voice, "Drew, they simply don't know any better."

That's why I wrote this book. To pierce the veil of silly nonsense and costly myths. To pull off the blinders worn by so many well-meaning but terribly misinformed businesspeople who are scratching their heads wondering why their crippled horses—their poorly constructed ads, brochures, sales letters, e-mails, and Websites—aren't winning races.

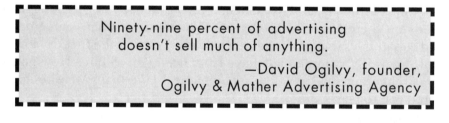

Ninety-nine percent of advertising doesn't sell much of anything.

—David Ogilvy, founder, Ogilvy & Mather Advertising Agency

How to Read This Book: Advice From the Masters

Some time ago, an American reporter traveled to Tibet to interview a wise old Zen master. When the two sat down for tea, instead of letting the Zen master do the talking, the reporter began to brag about all the things *he* knew about life!

The guy ranted on and on while the master poured the reporter's tea. As he endlessly babbled, the tea quickly rose to the rim of his cup and began spilling all over the floor. The reporter finally stopped yakking and said with surprise, "What are you doing? You can't pour in any more! The cup is overflowing!"

"Yes," responded the wise master. "This teacup, like your mind, is so full of ideas that there is no room for new information. You must first empty your head before any new knowledge can enter."

Be open to new ideas, but do not *believe* what I tell you.

Don't either *believe* or *disbelieve* what you read in this book. I don't even want you to accept what I say as *the* best way. And, most of all, please don't read this book and then say, "Wow! Drew Eric Whitman really knows his stuff!" and then sit down with a bag of chips and watch *Seinfeld* reruns.

Mere belief in these ideas won't put cash in your pockets. Belief alone won't put food on your table, clothes on your back, or a new car in your driveway. Instead, I want you to *experience* the results of *using* the techniques I share with you. Experience how your business and bank account grow. Experience the thrill of having an ever-increasing number of people hand you cash, write you checks, debit their credit cards, and pump up your PayPal account. How? By putting these principles into action.

No matter what you sell, I hope this book helps you succeed. If one day you can attribute even a tiny percentage of your success to what I've taught you, I will have succeeded as well.

Introduction

Would you like to learn dozens of little-known principles and techniques of advertising psychology used by the world's highest-paid copywriters and designers?

If you said yes, this book will open a whole new world for you. It will teach you secrets known only to the masters of persuasion, the ad-agency experts who know how to tap into people's innermost desires, and influence them to spend money. It will teach you what to do and how to do it.

Bottom line: This book will help you make more money.

And it doesn't matter if you sell aardvarks or zwieback cookies. Because I'm going to teach you—right here in these fast-moving pages—how to tap into the minds of your prospects like a highly paid consumer psychologist; like a supremely skilled ad-agency copywriter who knows (and uses) all the tricks of the trade to influence consumers to read their offers, and respond by pulling out their wallets.

Persuasion and Influence

Now, if these two words scare you, *stop reading here*. Really. It means this book is not for you. (I just used a technique on you. Keep reading and I'll teach you how to use it too.) You see, to many, these words conjure up thoughts of evildoers out to take advantage of the poor, unsuspecting public.

> Advertising is only evil when it advertises evil things.
> —David Ogilvy

The truth is, you and I are influenced by these techniques every day. And when used properly to advertise quality products and services, it's perfectly legal, ethical, and moral.

Question: When you walk into a car dealership, do you really think you're simply having an everyday chat with the sales rep? Sorry, you're not. A skilled salesperson is a master in psychological communication strategies. Chances are, *you* are not. And it's the salesperson's goal to move you from "looker" to "buyer."

You see, while you're shooting the breeze, admiring the beautiful, shiny paint, breathing in the aromatic leather upholstery, and drooling over the 550-horsepower engine, that "nice" salesperson is reading you like a book.

Like it or not, he's pulling you through a series of deliciously persuasive steps that are rapidly and continually being tailored to your every response—*and you're not even noticing!* (Why did I just say *pulling you* rather than *taking you*? Was it intentional? Oh yes. I'll explain in detail, later in this book.) If you say A, he'll say B. If instead you say C, he'll jump to D. There's little you can do to surprise him. He's seen it all before.

Listen: His goal is not to be your friend. It's also not to whittle away his day with pleasant chatter. His goal is for you to sign a hardcore, legally binding contract—the act that puts money in his pocket and food on his table.

But don't be alarmed: That's what sales is all about, of course! And if you're happy with your purchase, maybe you'll buy your next car from him. (Chances are he won't have to work as hard the second time.)

Likewise, advertising's purpose is not to entertain, but to persuade consumers to part with billions of dollars every day in exchange for products and services. And much like you in that car dealership, most consumers know nothing about the intensive research and psychological methodology that lie behind those ads! Guess what. They're not supposed to.

Those commercials you see and hear on TV and radio are more than just a collection of words and sounds. They are elegant amalgams of communication strategies designed to move you from your current mindset of a looker to that of a buyer.

Did you know that teams of skilled consumer psychologists routinely consult with ad agencies to help them construct ads that powerfully affect consumers on a psychological, even subconscious level? It's true! But don't be alarmed...that's what advertising is all about! And if you're happy with your purchase, maybe you'll buy again.

You see, advertising is a subset of communication.

Sales is a subset of advertising.

Persuasion is a subset of sales.

And psychology is a subset of persuasion.

Each is a form of the other, and it all leads back to psychology: the study of the human mind.

"But I just want to keep the good citizens informed, Drew! I don't want to influence or persuade anyone!" Hogwash! And I'll prove it.

Let's assume you own a pizza shop. (The same holds true no matter what kind of business you operate: real estate, physician, attorney, roofer, Web consultant, contractor, whatever.) If you *really* don't want to persuade anyone, then why aren't you running ads that simply state what you sell, the price, and your address, Website, and phone number, like this:

GIUSEPPE SELLS PIZZA: $9.99. 123 Mozzarella Road.

www.BigCheeseDisk.com (800)123-4567.

You wouldn't do it on your life! Why not? I'll tell you.

Because you don't dare want the prospects to make up their *own* minds as to whether or not they want to buy your pizzas. You'd much rather make their minds up for them! (That's persuasion.) You'd rather *tell* them how to feel about your pizza. (That's influence.) The result being that they buy, buy, buy. (The end result of that persuasion and influence.)

Studying psychology to boost the effectiveness of your ads isn't evil. It simply teaches you:

1. What people want.
2. How they feel about what they want.
3. Why they act as they do.

And once you know this, you can:

1. Better understand how to satisfy your customers.
2. Influence more people to buy.
3. Get your quality products into more people's hands.
4. Help add more satisfaction to their lives.

See? It's not so bad after all, is it? Not if you start with a quality product. Of course, influencing more people to buy a crummy product that typically self-destructs within the first week of ownership is something else. You don't need psychology. You need a shot of ethics.

Above all, if you suffer from being too timid in your advertising—as are most advertisers today—this book will give you a giant boot in the pants. Ready to dig in? Let's go!

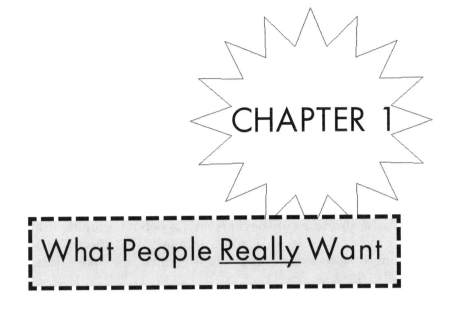

CHAPTER 1

What People <u>Really</u> Want

Born in 1883, Daniel Starch was considered the nation's leading advertising and marketing psychologist. His publication *Starch Advertising Readership Reports* opened people's eyes wide. Why? Because his writings showed advertisers how much money they were flushing down the toilet.

"Think your ad is great?" he said, in so many words, to big magazine advertisers around the country. "Your 'oh-so-great' ads are ignored by more than half of everyone who reads the magazines!" he blasted.

"How could this be?" the ad men puzzled. "Our ads are marvelous...they show our entire factory, and all our wonderful equipment from several really unusual camera-angles, and tell about our incredible products!"

Starch blasted them again: "Guess what guys? People *couldn't care less* about your smoke-belching factories! They don't give a *damn* about how many people you have on staff, or how many square feet your company occupies. And they don't give a flying flounder how fancy your equipment is, or your—*gasp!*—'unusual camera angles,' or *any* of that other self-serving junk!"

Instead, Starch's research showed that people care mostly about is (get ready for this earth-shaking revelation)...*themselves*!

They care about what products will *do* for them, how they'll make their lives better, happier, more fulfilled. What a revelation! But isn't this common sense? Doesn't *every* advertiser know this today? Ha! How foolish of us to think so.

Just look around you. Look at today's newspaper and magazine ads. Check out TV and radio commercials. Surf the Web and look in your e-mail in-box. You'll find that what you and I might think was common sense...is apparently *not*.

Decades have passed since Daniel Starch issued his initial findings. Yesterday's advertising researchers are probably screaming from their graves today: "Haven't you learned a thing?! We dedicated *years* to re-searching how to make your bank accounts grow like Jack's freaky beanstalk. *Open your eyes!*"

Sigh. It's frustrating. The truth is, they haven't learned a thing. Most (yes, most) of today's advertisers still haven't learned the basic lesson: people don't care about you, they care first about themselves.

In 1935, H.E. Warren wrote an article entitled "How to Understand Why People Buy," which every advertiser and salesperson should read twice. He said:

> To understand why people buy, we...should know people and have a keen sense of human nature. We should know how people think...how people live, and be acquainted with the standards and customs affecting their everyday lives.... We should fully know their needs and their wants and be able to distinguish between the two. An understanding of why people buy is gained by a willingness to acquire proved and tested principles of commercial psychology to selling.

Okay, enough background. Let's jump in. First, I'll teach you the 17 foundational principles of consumer psychology. Once you understand how they work, I'll teach you 41 easy-to-use, little-known response-boosting advertising techniques. Many of these will incorporate one or more of the 17 principles, and others will introduce you to psychologi-cal theories specific to advertising writing and design. Best of all, I'll tell you how to use them in your own promotions to help light a fire under your sales curve.

Forget everything else. Here's what people *really* want.

Consumer researchers and psychologists know what people want. They should—they've studied the subject for years. And although all researchers don't agree completely with every finding, there are eight foundational "desires" common to everyone.

I call them the *Life-Force 8* (LF8 for short). These eight powerful desires are responsible for more sales than all other human wants combined. Here they are. Learn them. Use them. Profit from them.

The Life-Force 8

Human beings are *biologically programmed* with the following eight desires:

1. Survival, enjoyment of life, life extension.
2. Enjoyment of food and beverages.
3. Freedom from fear, pain, and danger.
4. Sexual companionship.
5. Comfortable living conditions.
6. To be superior, winning, keeping up with the Joneses.
7. Care and protection of loved ones.
8. Social approval.

Who could argue with these things? We *all* want them, don't we? But in how many of *your* ads do you openly use an appeal to one or more of the LF8? I bet few, if any. Why am I such a doubting Thomas? Simply because it's unlikely that anyone ever taught you to do so.

Listen: When you create an advertising appeal based on any of the LF8, you tap into the power of Mother Nature herself. You tap into the very essence of what makes humans tick. You see, you can't escape your desires for the LF8. You were born with them, and they'll be with you until the day you die. For example:

* Can you shake your desire to eat? (LF8 #2)
* Can you suppress your will to survive? (LF8 #1)
* How easily can you quash your desire for physical comfort? (LF8 #5)
* Can you stop caring whether or not your child looks both ways before crossing the street? (LF8 #7)

You don't need to conduct studies to answer these questions; the answers are obvious. These desires are biologically programmed in each of us. They're part of what makes us human. They're powerful motivators. And smart advertisers can tap into them like pushing a plug into an outlet.

What Can You Learn About
Desire From a Master Bookseller?

When it came to making big money selling books, mail order guru Haldeman-Julius *wrote* the book. During the 1920s and '30s he sold more than 200 million of them, in nearly 2,000 different titles. They were simple little books, and they all cost just 5 cents each. To advertise his books, he placed ads consisting of only the books' titles. If a book didn't sell well, he'd change the ad copy, but not the way you'd expect. He actually changed the titles of the books! Then he'd sit back and study the response. How clever.

Look what happened when the titles were changed based on the LF8.

Old Title	Annual Sales	New Title	Annual Sales & LF8 Affected
Ten O'Clock	2,000	What Art Should Mean to You	9,000 (LF#8)
Fleece of Gold	5,000	Quest for a Blonde Mistress	50,000 (LF#4)
Art of Controversy	0	How to Argue Logically	30,000 (LF#6)
Casanova and His Loves	8,000	Casanova, History's Greatest Lover	22,000 (LF#4)
Apothegems	2,000	Truth About the Riddle of Life	9,000 (LF#1)

According to Haldeman-Julius, the two strongest appeals were *sex* and *self-improvement*. Surprised? Neither am I. So again I ask you: How many of *your* current ads contain either of these appeals? When you tap into these innate desires, you harness the unstoppable momentum of the emotions that drive people every second of every day.

> People buy because of emotion and justify
> with logic. Force an emotional response by
> touching on a basic want or need.
> —"Seven Principles of Stopping Power,"
> The Young & Rubicam Traveling Creative Workshop

The Nine Learned (Secondary) Human Wants

Perhaps you read the list of eight primary wants and thought, "Heck, I want more than just these eight things!" Of course you do. We have many other wants. We want to look good, and be healthy, well educated, effective, and so on. (Don't you?) These are called *secondary*, or *learned wants*, and nine have been identified:

1. To be informed.
2. Curiosity.
3. Cleanliness of body and surroundings.
4. Efficiency.
5. Convenience.
6. Dependability/quality.
7. Expression of beauty and style.
8. Economy/profit.
9. Bargains.

These secondary wants are strong, but they don't even come close to the LF8. They're way in the background, completely clouded by your LF8 dust. We're not born with these secondary wants. We *learned* them. They're not hard-wired in our brains as are the LF8. Used as tools of influence, they're not as bankable as the LF8 because we're not biologically driven to satisfy them. (Read that again.) And when it comes to human desires, biology is king. There's nothing more powerful than tapping into a desire that you can't shake. It's like jumping onto a speeding train: Once you're on, you don't need to lift a finger to get it moving— you're already flying along!

Think about it. Which desire would you respond to first: to buy a new shirt, or to run out of a burning building? If you're single, would you be more driven to organize your desk or have amazing sex with the hottie whose been flirting with you at lunch every day? Would you first

23

protect your spouse from a crazed attacker, or ignore the assault and instead go shopping for wallpaper for your guest bathroom? The answers are obvious. And the interesting thing about the LF8 is that we don't even know—or ever question—these desires. We simply *want* them—no, we *must* have them. We can't shake them no matter what we do. Again, they're hardwired into us. These examples should give you a better idea why the LF8 are so powerful, and why using them in your ads can be so effective: You'll be tapping into the human psyche, the core programming of the human brain itself.

But what exactly *is* desire? It's a type of tension you feel when a need isn't met. If you're hungry, for example, the tension to eat arises and the desire for food (LF8 #2) kicks in. If you see a creepy-looking middle-aged guy chatting online with your 8-year-old daughter, the tension to protect your child arises and your desire to start monitoring her internet usage (LF8 #7) kicks in. If your office chair breaks your back after just 10 minutes of use, the tension to be comfortable arises, and your desire to buy a new chair (LF8 #5) kicks in.

So here's the simple formula for desire, and the result it sets in motion:

Tension → Desire → Action to Satisfy the Desire

In short, when you appeal to people's LF8 desires, you create a drive that motivates them to take an action that will fulfill that desire as soon as possible.

Now here's an especially interesting fact, of particular importance to us advertisers. Not only is it pleasant for us to satisfy our eight primary desires, but it's also pleasant for us to *read* about how *others* have satisfied them. It's a form of vicarious LF8 desire fulfillment. Fascinating, isn't it?

For example, by reading how consumer George Vincent was able to pay off all his debts using a radical new approach to real estate investing, you and I—on the giant projector screen of our minds—envision a brilliantly clear, superbly detailed account of *ourselves* paying off all *our* bills, laughing as we dash off checks to *our* creditors in a devil-may-care fashion, leaning back in our big leather chair, throwing our feet up on our desk, and enjoying a debt-free, piles-of-cash-in-the-bank lifestyle.

Sounds great, doesn't it? But did you see what I just did? By using language that's both *specific* and *visual*, I was able to install a *mental movie* inside your head. We'll explore these mental movies in more detail in Chapter 3, in Ad Agency Secret #18: Directing Mental Movies.

But for now, just know that by using specific visual words, you can give your audience a sense of what it's like to actually interact with your product or enjoy the benefits of your service—to demonstrate its use inside their minds—long before they actually buy it. This vicarious pleasure is where the persuasion begins, because *the first use of any product is inside the consumers' minds*. (Stop. Read that last sentence again.) Imagining the use of something that appeals to you increases your desire for it.

For example, let's say you love ice cream. If you spend all afternoon thinking about ordering a giant hot fudge sundae at dinner with three giant scoops of Guittard mint chocolate chip, two big ladles of steaming, extra-dark hot fudge, chopped wet nuts, all blanketed in a cloud of fluffy whipped cream with a maraschino cherry on top, you're naturally going to want it more than if you hadn't thought about it. And ultimately— if that desire is strong enough—you'll take some form of action that results in your having mint chocolate chip ice cream, hot fudge, chopped nuts, and a maraschino cherry floating around in your stomach. (And perhaps some in your lap, too, if you're particularly exuberant while eating it.)

Again, notice how my choice of words causes you to imagine ice cream, nuts, steaming-hot fudge and a bright red cherry floating in your stomach. If I instead said, "you'll take some form of action that results in your having eaten it," your mental movie screen would have— *POOF!*—gone blank. And—this is critical—the less imagery you convey, the less your message occupies consumers' brains, the less likely it is that you'll influence them. Let me drive this point home with another example.

Let's look at transforming a bland sentence with no imagery power into a Hollywood blockbuster. The bland sentence is: "Go somewhere and do something." Yawn. Each successive variation of this sentence will build in visual intensity, not simply because we add words and sentences, but because the words I use are intentionally selected to install mental movies—visuals—in your head.

* Go somewhere and do something. (This is a blank movie screen. No imagery.)
* Go somewhere and *get* something. (*Do* can mean anything. *Get* is more specific.)
* Go to the *kitchen* and get something. (Still vague, but now you know where to go.)

✳ Go to the kitchen and get *food*. (Ahh, now we're getting somewhere. Do you see how filling in the details creates imagery?)

✳ Go to the kitchen, *open the oven*, and get food. (Notice how you pictured yourself opening an oven. Specific wording implants images. Action words create moving pictures.)

✳ Go to the kitchen, open the oven, and *pull out the pizza*. (Very visual. A picture of a pizza pops into your head, whether you want it to or not! See the power of this? You can't help but picture what I write about, if I use specific visual words.)

✳ Go to the kitchen, open the oven, and pull out the freshest, crispiest, most delicious hot pizza you've ever eaten. Go on, cut yourself a big, hearty slice. Careful, it's hot! Now take a big bite. Talk about crisp! The dough was made fresh this morning and baked in a virgin olive oil–coated black pan for a thick, deep-dish Chicago style crust. The sauce? Prepared from scratch, of course, from juicy plum tomatoes picked this morning, and blended with select fresh herbs from our own garden. Cheese? You betcha! Lots and lots of chewy, whole-milk mozzarella, made from the finest buffalo milk, of course, and the entire pie baked to bubbling perfection in a 750-degree wood-burning brick oven imported from Genoa, Italy. (Okay, I really maxed out this one to prove my point. And chances are you experienced a rich and detailed series of images by simply reading my words.)

We'll talk more about this whole business of using positive visual adjectives in Ad Agency Secret #17: PVAs—The Easy Way to Boost the Power of Your Copy. But for now, to sum up this chapter, just be aware of these five things:

1. People have eight basic wants—the LF8 (survival; food and drink; freedom from fear, pain, and danger; sexual companionship; comfortable living conditions; to be superior; care and protection of loved ones; and social approval).

2. The strongest advertising appeals are based on these eight basic wants.

3. The most effective way to create an appeal based on these eight wants is to write ad copy that causes your prospects to *visually* demonstrate your product or service inside their heads, sufficiently enough to build desire for the satisfaction of the want(s) that your product promises to provide...and then to choose your product to attain it.

4. Now that you've got them wanting fulfillment, your next job is to influence them to believe that your product actually delivers what you say. It's *credibility* time, and we'll discuss this in Ad Agency Technique #15: The Psychology of "Social Proof," and Ad Agency Technique #33: Guarantees that Guarantee Higher Response.

5. They believe you. They want it. Yippee! Time to count your money, right? *Wrong!* You now have to push them to *act*. We'll discuss how to do this in Ad Agency Technique #19: Battling Human Inertia. And I'll give you a slew of quick tips in the following Chapter 4 Hot List sections: "22 Response Superchargers," "13 Ways to Make Buying Easy," and "11 Ways to Boost Coupon Returns."

Let's now look at the 17 foundational principles of consumer psychology. In Chapter 2, I teach you what they are, why they work, and how you can use them to help sell *your* products and services.

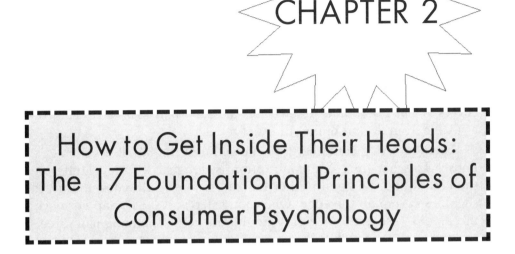

How to Get Inside Their Heads: The 17 Foundational Principles of Consumer Psychology

Principle #1: The Fear Factor— *Selling the Scare*

Fact: Your home is a cesspool filled with hundreds of strains of evil bacteria waiting to infect your innocent child as he crawls along the kitchen floor, sticking plastic toy blocks into his mouth. Don't laugh. Did you know that one single bacteria cell explodes into more than 8 *million* cells in less than 24 hours? And that invisible microbes of all kinds can cause everything from athlete's foot to diarrhea, the common cold to the flu, meningitis, pneumonia, sinusitis, skin diseases, strep throat, tuberculosis, urinary tract infections, and a lot more.

The solution? Lysol® Disinfectant Spray. It quickly kills 99.9 percent of germs on commonly touched surfaces throughout the home. And it's only about $5 a can.

Fact: No matter how often you wash your sheets, your bed is an insect breeding ground, teeming with thousands of hideous, crab-like dust mites aggressively laying eggs in your pillow and mattress, causing you and your family to suffer year-long allergy attacks. While you sleep, they actually wake up and start to crawl, eat your skin flakes, and drink the moisture on your flesh. *It gets worse.* Did you know that 10 percent of the weight of a two-year-old pillow is actually dead mites and their feces? This means that every night you and your family are sleeping in the equivalent of an insect's toilet, actually covered in a mélange of both their living and dead bodies, and oceans of their bitter excrement.

The solution? Bloxem® anti-mite mattress covers and pillow cases help reduce allergy symptoms associated with dust mite infestation. The special fabric's tightly crafted pores don't allow microscopic mites to enter your mattress, nest, and breed. Your family enjoys a more peaceful night's rest. And they're so affordable: Bloxem anti-mite mattress covers are just $60, and pillow cases are less than $10 each. They're available from dozens of fine Internet retailers.

Fact: Your dog could be the next victim of the horrible groomer's noose! This hangman-like contraption is designed to keep Fluffy on the table while she's getting her haircut. It's perfectly safe—that is, if she doesn't step off the edge! One wrong step and she'd snap her neck like an old-west bandit swinging from branches of the hangman's tree.

The solution? Call Vanity 'n' Fur groomers, where we use loving kindness to beautify your doggie, never dangerous mechanical contraptions—like the groomer's noose—that less-experienced groomers risk using everyday.

Bottom line: *Fear sells.* It motivates. It urges. It moves people to action. It drives them to spend money. In fact, social psychologists and consumer researchers have been studying its effects for more than 50 years. Whether it's selling a loaf of bread, which hardly seems scary (until you show them studies reporting that refined white flour may cause cancer), or painting a picture of doom and gloom about the insidious nature of odorless carbon monoxide creeping through air conditioning vents and wiping out their family (while *they're* sleeping safely in a hotel on a business trip), properly constructed, fear can move people to spend.

But *why* does it work? In a word: stress. Fear causes stress. And stress causes the desire to do something. Missing a big sale causes the stress of loss. Choosing the right tires can cause the stress of concern for personal safety. Not opting for the side-curtain airbags in your new car causes the stress of future regret and visions of physical injury. Fear suggests loss. Fear paints a picture of necessary response. It tells your prospect that he or she will be somehow damaged. This threatens the ego's continuous quest for self-preservation. Therefore, the threat of being damaged is insidious and powerful.

Can you use it for your products and services? Yes...if your product offers the appropriate solution for a fearful situation. But is it ethical?

Yes, but only if what you're selling offers a truly effective solution. Certain products *can* quell fears. And there's nothing wrong with promoting—and profiting—from them.

"Oh, Drew...that's so manipulative! Scaring people to buy! How could you?"

If you thought or said this statement, please read my Introduction again. I said that if using persuasion and influence scares you, you should stop reading. That's because there aren't enough pages in this book—nor is it my intention—to try to convince you of the *morality* of using a fear appeal. I mean, what could I possibly say to convince you that it's okay to use fear when selling your brake pad replacement service? (Isn't it obvious?) Or life insurance? Home smoke detectors? Cancer insurance? The mere mention of these things—to me, anyway—conjures up fearful situations that require some form of self-protection. If that form of self-protection presents itself via an advertiser who happens to be selling a product that can save my life, prevent pain, or otherwise help me better deal with an unpleasant situation, then I welcome it. I have no problem being informed, and swiftly moved to take caution. Do you?

Bottom line: if it's possible to use fear to effectively sell a product or service, it means that inherent in that product or service is the possible resolution to that which is feared. If not, no matter how much fear you try to conjure up, your appeal will fail miserably. Make sense?

The Four-Step Recipe for Inducing Fear

Okay, so you've determined that your product or service can genuinely alleviate a real fear-producing problem and is a good candidate for using the fear appeal. In order to make it work, there's a specific, four-ingredient recipe you must follow.

In their study, *Age of Propaganda* (2001), Pratkanis and Aronson argue that, "the fear appeal is most effective when:

1. It scares the hell out of people.
2. It offers a specific recommendation for overcoming the fear-aroused threat.
3. The recommended action is perceived as effective for reducing the threat.
4. The message recipient believes that he or she can perform the recommended action."

The success or failure of this strategy relies on the existence of *all four* components. Remove any one of them, and it's like building your own computer and leaving out the hard drive. No matter how much you want it to work, it simply won't compute!

What's more, if you create too much fear, you could actually scare someone to *inaction*, like a deer, staring frozen into the headlights of an oncoming SUV. Fear can paralyze. And it will motivate your prospect to act only if he believes he has the power to *change* his situation. That means in order to craft an effective fear appeal, your ad must contain *specific, believable recommendations* for reducing the threat that are both credible and achievable.

For example, let's say you own a karate school and you're selling self-defense training. You can teach people to walk even the roughest streets with the confidence of a trained bodyguard, ready to counter even the most vicious attacks by the scariest (and ugliest) thugs walking the earth. Fact is, you need to do more than simply present gruesome crime stats. You must also convince your prospect that it's within her ability—using your system—to fight off an attacker using her bare hands. Ignore this vital step, and all you've accomplished is scaring her. You must also *convince* her, using factors that boost credibility (testimonials, video demonstrations, free lessons, and other believability boosters that we'll discuss later), and open her mind to the *possibility* that your claim is true, and that she really *can* enjoy the benefits you're promising. (She *wants* to believe you, because you're making an appealing claim. It's your job to help her believe you, and that takes more than simply shouting "boo!")

The fear appeal is also more successful if the fears targeted are *specific* and *widely recognized*. It's a lot easier to sell your sunscreen because *everyone* knows the sun can fry you like bacon and turn your skin into a melanoma factory. It's much tougher to sell laundry detergent that helps prevent ultraviolet damage to *clothing*. Why? Because few people are concerned with UV laundry damage. When's the last time this issue kept *you* awake? Although the fear *is* specific (damage to clothing), it's certainly not widely recognized.

Listen: Your goal is not to create *new* fears, but to tap into *existing* fears, either those on the forefront of consumers' minds, or those that require a little digging to uncover.

For example, take what I affectionately call "germ gel." You may know it as Purell Instant Hand Sanitizer, the leading brand. I don't go anywhere without it. In fact, if I leave the house and forget my small bottle, I'm thrown into somewhat of a panic. Why is this? GOJO Industries— the company that manufactures the germ-quashing goop—first introduced Purell to the food service and healthcare industries in 1988. Thinking back to that time—and even before—I don't recall ever feeling creeped out about touching things in public the way I do today. Sure, I was always health conscious; I always washed my hands before eating, and throughout the day as needed. I knew germs existed everywhere. And yet, the "need" to keep my hands relatively germ-free was simply not a concern back then. It wasn't on the forefront of my mind.

Jump ahead to 1997, when Purell hit the consumer market. *Aha!* Did you know that unwashed hands are the leading cause of food contamination in restaurants? Hand-washing? What a joke! A 2003 survey sponsored by the American Society of Microbiology (ASM) found that many people passing through major U.S. airports don't wash their hands after using the public facilities. More than 30 percent of people using restrooms in New York airports, 19 percent of those in Miami's airport, and 27 percent of air travelers at Chicago's O'Hare aren't stopping to wash their hands. In a phone survey the same year conducted by Wirthlin Worldwide, only 58 percent of people say they wash their hands after sneezing or coughing, and only 77 percent say they wash their hands after changing a diaper.

In 1972, the Journal of the American Medical Association described a study wherein they cultured bacteria from 200 coins and bills and found fecal bacteria and Staphylococcus aureus on 13 percent of coins and 42 percent of notes. It concluded: "Money is truly dirty." Heck, visit Purell.com and you'll see their list of "99.99 Germy Reasons to Use Purell."

Listerine created a shockwave of paranoia with the distasteful word *halitosis* in 1900. The copywriter for antiperspirant Odorno (what a name!) caused ladies to question their "daintiness" with a groundbreaking headline in the 1919 *Ladies Home Journal* that read, "In the Curve of a Woman's Arm." GOJO did the same for bacteria. *They made it an issue.* Something to think—and fret—about. They instilled fear. And, as a result, Listerine now boasts an impressive 53 percent market share. Odorno boosted sales 112 percent using that poetic headline (despite causing 200 women to cancel their subscriptions out of sheer disgust with the suggestion that they'd need such a product). And today, GOJO's Purell is the largest-selling brand of instant hand sanitizer, causing countless germaphobes to carry the stuff around in their handy travel bottle holders that attach conveniently to their key chains. (See how they made it easy to resolve the fear?)

A common way fear is used to simulate action is via the use of *deadlines* and *scarcity*. Phrases and slogans such as *limited offer, one-day sale,* and *while supplies last* have the effect of scaring consumers into believing that unless they act now, they'll miss a fantastic opportunity to save money, tapping into Human Secondary Want #9. The deadline tactic follows the guidelines by offering the consumer the means to address the "threat" by rushing out to purchase before it's too late.

However, fear is not a magical wand. It's not enough to simply scare someone, say a few nice things about your product, and sit back and wait for an onslaught of orders. Fear is simply one way to motivate your prospects to investigate your product further. Get it? You still need to *convince* him that *your* product provides the solution to the fear you just instilled. You still need to *persuade* and *motivate* him to take action: to grab his wallet, visit your Website, or call your 800 number and place his order. Don't fret! I'll teach you how to do all these things—and much more—in Chapter 3, where we discuss 41 advertising-specific techniques that incorporate many of the psychological principles we're now reviewing.

Principle #2: Ego Morphing— *Instant Identification*

When you see the Marlboro man, it's your *ego*—not your craving for paper tubes stuffed with tobacco—that motivates you to switch brands.

When you see the Victoria's Secret models with their long, silky hair and piercing eyes slinking around in their lacy undergarments, it's your *ego*, not your admiration for the directorial style of the commercial, that motivates you to buy the slinkwear.

The fact is, you can blame your ego for many of your high credit card bills.

The foundation for Ego Morphing and the Vanity Appeal was described by Pratkanis and Aronson (*Age of Propaganda*, 1991), when they said, "By purchasing the 'right stuff,' we [the consumer] enhance our own egos and rationalize away our inadequacies."

Imagine that! We can actually buy things to make up for what we believe is a lacking in our personalities. You've heard of *retail therapy*, right? Could it be that we as advertisers are actually performing a function more vital than simply providing people with goods and services? Could it be that we're actually assisting in our customers' psychological development as well?

In reality, this technique allows you to create a certain image, or identity, for a product, in order to appeal to a particular section of the audience that feels that their personal image and ego either match it or could be improved by it.

Your goal is to cause consumers to become so closely associated with the product's image that it almost becomes a part of their own identity; thus, you're "morphing" their ego to fit your product. By representing your product through carefully chosen images and personalities, you can persuade your prospects that, by purchasing or using your wares, they'll immediately become associated with these images and attitudes.

Persuading this way is not difficult. You don't have to work hard to persuade a woman to want to be sexier and more in control, or for a man to be more powerful, self-confident, and appealing to women. These things are built in, pre-wired into our very being. And because the majority of *true* prospects for your product already believe they possess the ideas and values associated with it—or have the desire to develop them (otherwise they wouldn't be *true* prospects)—you're actually tapping into this pre-wiring. Don't you see? You're selling an easy route to fulfill what we know they *already* want more of. And for those who believe they already have it, our product can help them too, by giving them a way to express what they feel about themselves to the outside world.

What does all this mean? Simply that you can appeal to your audience's vanity and ego without the need for persuasive ideas or evidence by concentrating on showing your prospects the images they want to see. For example, start noticing how very little persuasive copy is used in ads for luxury goods. They're "feel good" ads. They present an image that's carefully crafted to evoke the emotional response of *desire*—for the item advertised. Here's an example of the elaborate and complex purchase decision pattern when such an ad is viewed by a true prospect:

"Oooooh, look at these hot-looking girls climbing all over that guy wearing those kewl Hollister jeans. I want those jeans."

Don't laugh. That's about it all it takes. And if it didn't work, retailers such as Hollister and Abercrombie & Fitch wouldn't be spending a fortune placing such ads. (Nor would Lexus, BMW, Jaguar, and high-end-product advertisers of most every kind. Oh, did I mention Rolls-Royce? Yeah, them too.)

Does it work? Consider the perfume and cologne business. Aside from impregnating paper flaps with their product so people can take a whiff, the only thing these advertisers do to persuade their prospects to buy is show photos of hot-looking women and men whom we're supposed to believe are customers. The models aren't even wearing the perfumes and colognes during the photo shoot! So really, 99.9 percent of the ad has nothing to do with the products being promoted. It's pure imagery. But manufacturers apparently know it works: 2008 cologne sales are expected to reach $1.6 billion. Women's fragrances? Add another $3.2 billion.

Appealing to people's vanity and ego is most successful when it hones in on characteristics that society considers being desirable, such as physical attractiveness, intelligence, economic success, and sexual prowess. As suggested by Stec and Bernstein's *Balance Theory* (1999), if consumers are presented with the "correct" images, people who possess these characteristics will buy them in order to publicize their ego. Those who don't will purchase them in an attempt to *appear* as if they do. Interesting, isn't it?

So think about your product. Does owning or using it suggest qualities that people would want to flaunt? You own a karate school? Then spotlight the names of the big mixed martial arts stars who work out there. Then print and sell T-shirts that say "I train with [insert big-name star here]." Instant ego appeal.

You're the most expensive dog groomer in town? Show photos of the rich celebrities who bring in their pooches. Feature Mr. or Ms. Celeb stepping out of a limo with a drooling pooch. "Oh, yes...there are plenty of other groomers in town, but pshaw! I only trust the Karringtons with *my* Fluffy." So snotty, but—BOOM!—instant ego appeal.

You're a printer specializing in high-end stationery and wedding invitations? Brag about the well-known personalities who've used your services. Huh? You say there *are* no well-known personalities who've used your services? That's an easy fix. Offer to do a free job for a few of your favorite local celebs—newscasters, or social and political leaders, for example. When they accept, send them 250 letterheads and envelopes on your finest paper...then drop some names as to whose stationery you've printed. Voila! Instant ego appeal.

You're a security firm? What big companies (that have far more rigorous security requirements than your typical prospect) trust you to protect them? Say, "Why Do More Local Bank Presidents Choose FortKnox Security to Protect Their Own Homes Than Anyone Else?" And then, the variation: "Why Do More Local Jewelry Store Owners Choose FortKnox Security to Protect Their Homes Than Anyone Else?"

Get it? If bank presidents and jewelry store owners trust you to protect their family and their biggest investment (their home), then, as the average prospect, I'd feel good about hiring you to secure *my* modest home. Doing so puts me in the company of these discerning executives. Again, instant ego appeal.

Back to Rolls-Royce.

Question: Would such a distinguished British automaker—long before they were gobbled up by BMW and Volkswagen—stoop to engaging in such a "manipulative" ploy?

Answer: Is a bullfrog waterproof?

Imagine a full-page magazine ad consisting of little more than one large photo of what looks like a Manhattan intersection. From our bird's-eye view, we see a driver patiently waiting for the light to change. The ridiculously shiny black convertible Rolls-Royce with Sir Charles Sykes's internationally recognized silvery winged mascot, "The Spirit of Ecstasy," declares the owner's good taste and insistence on excellence. Well dressed in business attire, he appears to be about 55 years old, salt-and-pepper hair, confident and relaxed, an executive of some type, no doubt, thinking a myriad of "all is right with the world"-type thoughts, staring straight ahead. To the left of his car, we see another driver of about the same age, the entire weight of his head resting in his left hand, looking enviously at the driver in the Rolls. Feeling on top of the world just moments before Mr. RR pulled up, he's now squirming uncomfortably...in his *Mercedes*. Match point, game over.

Not all businesses can use such an ego-driven approach. The nature of all products and services doesn't dictate such a prescription. Fret not. There are plenty of other techniques that will fit your product or service just fine.

Like a sharpshooter peering through a rifle scope, the techniques we've discussed so far target your prospects' internal attitudes and innate psychological hot buttons. The following technique influences consumer behavior by associating products and services with symbols of authority or reverence.

Principle #3: Transfer—*Credibility by Osmosis*

"I don't understand!" shouted the advertiser. "That's the best damned ad I've ever written! Look at that beautiful layout! Look at that gorgeous photo! My price is right and I make it easy for people to order. This newspaper has an excellent circulation so I know I'm reaching my audience. And," he continues, "it's a product that would really help people! So why isn't anyone ordering?"

The problem? Nobody *believes* him.

That's right. No matter how wonderful your ad, brochure, sales letter, Web page, e-mail, or radio or TV commercial, if your prospects don't believe you, you've flushed your ad money down the toilet. Your offer *must* be credible, or you should expect the same crummy results as our frustrated advertiser friend here.

Transfer is a strategy that involves using symbols, images, or ideas—*cues*, if you will—commonly associated with people, groups, or institutions of authority or respect, in order to persuade your prospect that your product or service is in some way acceptably endorsed. And if something is endorsed by a person or group you respect, lights flash, bells ring, your brain spits out "instant credibility!" And if it's something you want and can afford, you'll start digging for your Visa card.

Socialization ensures that most people respect institutions such as the Church, the medical establishment, national agencies, and science. When you incorporate images or symbols from any of these groups into your ads, the trust you gain can offset your need to present as rigorous a persuasive argument. The ideal strategy? Get a respected institution to provide its official endorsement. Doing so instantly transfers their authority, sanction, and prestige to your product or service.

For example, let's say you're not sure which way to vote on a costly new crime bill that's up on referendum. It sounds good, but you don't know if it'll really make a difference on the street, where it matters most. Alas, a direct mail flyer from the Fraternal Order of Police lands in your mailbox. It says that they wholeheartedly support the bill and request your support in urging your state and local politicians to vote yes on its passage. Because you've always respected the organization, and even donated a few bucks to it, you're now far more likely to support the cause. "If the *police* like it," you reason, "it's good enough for me." And you're also likely to think—consciously or otherwise—"I respect the F.O.P. so I'm sure they've checked it out thoroughly. I'll vote yes."

Did you see what happened? Human inertia, a metaphor for *laziness*, leads you to rationalize not doing your own in-depth research. It's as simple as that.

Proactiv is just one of dozens of acne products being hawked today. However, it's the only one featuring singer Jessica Simpson testifying to its effectiveness. To young girls suffering from the skin condition, this is all the endorsement they need.

Quaker Oats enjoyed excellent growth of its product ever since it trademarked its first smiling Quaker man logo back in 1877. Unfortunately, 113 years later, in 1990, the *New England Journal of Medicine* released the controversial Sachs study that disputed claims that oats and oat bran could reduce cholesterol. Fortunately, Quaker had already launched a new campaign featuring actor Wilford Brimley in 1987. His disarming, down-to-earth straight talk and no-nonsense, "high-credibility demeanor" proclaimed the virtues of the flattened oats, and Quaker enjoyed a reversal of a 5-year sales decline.

If you can't get a *full* endorsement—a testimonial, for example—you can achieve similar success by spotlighting readily recognized symbols that carry the weight of endorsement.

Consider the Good Housekeeping Seal of Approval. This unassuming oval has instilled pre-purchase confidence in millions of consumers since 1909. A clever concept, the seal is awarded only to those products whose ads have been reviewed and accepted for publication in *Good Housekeeping* magazine. The publisher promises a refund or replacement for defective products within two years of purchase. Not only is this a great added-value inducement to buy ad space in *Good Housekeeping*, but it's also an ideal example of how a trusted group's symbol can give your prospect a sense of security before whipping out the cash. Just as any other guarantee, it could actually help you close the sale if you construct it properly. (More about guarantees later.)

I recently created a jumbo postcard for a hypnotist client. His prospects aren't familiar with any hypnosis-industry organizations, but the mere addition of the official-looking logo of the National Guild of Hypnotists is enough to suggest that my client's membership in the organization suggests the validity of his credentials, experience, and effectiveness. Now think. Do they really *mean* any of that? Of course not. Your prospects often use a *peripheral*, or noncritical style of thinking. It's this same "short-cut to persuasion" at work when we use symbols that connote—or denote—authority, agreement, acceptance, or recognition. Interestingly enough, I bet not 1 in 100 people who received my client's postcard had ever heard of the National Guild of Hypnotists. But thanks to the peripheral route to persuasion, it doesn't matter. It's all most consumers need for the added boost of confidence they need.

To simplify, here's what happens. Your prospects: 1) See a symbol of credibility (logo, endorsement, and the like), and then (2) question less of your sales argument.

Using generally accepted images of medical and scientific authority could also produce the transfer effect. Studies performed by the Institute for Propaganda Analysis suggest that from the simple image of an "expert" in a white lab coat showing medical stats, advertisers can tap the public's acceptance of physicians to influence consumer behavior, either for or against a product. Is it any wonder that so many ads for health products feature dignified-looking men in white lab jackets? Instant credibility! These advertisers know that you'll likely *transfer* your feelings about physicians to their product. It's a predictable one-two punch that works most every time.

"Okay Drew, enough examples. What do I *do* with this info?"

Simple. Think about which person, persons, and organizations in your industry have a reputation that carries sufficient respect that if you got them to endorse your business, product, or service, you could capitalize on the transfer of credibility it would create. For specifics about how to do this, see Ad Agency Technique #15: The Psychology of Social Proof, later in this book.

As the transfer technique shows, strategies that appeal to a broad range of the population can be highly successful. Next, let's explore a technique of *group persuasion*.

Principle #4: The Bandwagon Effect— *Give Them Something to Jump On*

Fact: Humans are social beings with a powerful psychological need to belong.

Long ago, our ancestors understood that, in order to maximize their chances for survival, it was in their best interests to form groups of like-minded individuals. So they lived in groups, hunted in groups, protected each other in groups. Everyone had a vital role that contributed to the success of the entire tribe. When the group ate, you ate. When it slept, you slept. When it packed up and moved, you moved. If it died...well, you get the picture.

Although modern societies no longer live this way, membership in—and identification with—*some* group is still critically important for our happiness. We have a need for friends, a romantic relationship, and, ultimately, marriage and children. We join social clubs, fraternities, and sororities; participate in community events; attend religious services; and form business organizations and even street gangs. Heck, we often wear shirts and caps proclaiming our associations, which makes us feel accepted, valuable, and important.

In fact, according to psychologist Abraham Maslow's well-known Hierarchy of Human Needs pyramid, the need to belong is third only to our physiological needs (food, clothing, and shelter) and our safety needs (security, stability, and freedom from fear). Once these first two needs have been satisfied, belonging or love—which is usually found within families, friendships, membership in associations, and within our community—becomes a top priority. It's another LF8 need that's hard-wired in us. And it's yet another handle the savvy advertiser can grip in order to persuade.

Three Types of Groups

Psychologists tell us there are three primary types of groups, regardless of the group's purpose:

1. Aspirational—Groups to which you'd *like* to belong.
2. Associative—Groups that *share* your ideals and values.
3. Dissociative—Groups to which you do *not* want to belong.

By linking products and services to any of these three reference groups, you can persuade your prospects to make decisions based upon the group with which they identify, or *want* to identify.

This strategy uses the *peripheral*—superficial thought—route to persuasion. (Remember we discussed this earlier?) That's because the consumer's purchase is based primarily on his or her sense of belonging, and not entirely on the merits of your product. The need for group membership is a strong psychological drive, and in its pursuit, most consumers will forego the need for an active, deep analysis of what you're selling. Aha! We've found yet another shortcut to persuasion.

And it's more than just something that just *sounds* good. It's backed by sound research. Stec and Bernstein (1999) support this strategy with their Consensus-Implies-Correctness heuristic, which claims that this psychological concept causes a "bandwagon" effect, which ensures that

41

-- --

if a large enough group holds a favorable opinion about a product, then that opinion must be correct. We'll discuss this finding in Principle #17.

But to which group do you attempt to link your prospects? Here's a rule of thumb: If seeking *aspirational* group influence—people your prospects aspire to be similar to—you must make sure your prospects can easily identify with them.

For example: Let's say you're selling a new style of bicycle seat for racing enthusiasts that feels as though you're floating on a cushion of air, rather than sitting on an agonizing platform of blunt, chisel-tip pallet nails. Research tells you that the median age of your target market is 34 years. This immediately tells you that it wouldn't be wise to feature a bunch of old men or women in your ad. You also don't want to show casual "Everyday Joe" riders on their way to a family picnic lunch. Likewise, your main photo shouldn't be of an unknown bicycler—even if he or she is your best customer who happens to spend $1,000 in parts and service every month.

Why? Well, remember the group label *aspirational*? These simply aren't the people your hardcore group *aspires* to emulate. Your audience doesn't want to be the guy or gal next door. They aspire to be similar to tour-winning legends Lance Armstrong, Miguel Indurain, or Eddy Merckx—three of the best cyclists of all time. Featuring pros such as these encourages your prospects to believe that, by using your cushy-soft seat, they can be more similar to their two-wheeled heroes.

Successfully gaining *associative* group influence is more complex. This strategy requires that you link your product to a certain societal group, while often alienating others. This can be done in two ways, either by (1) closely associating your product with the target group through advertising that specifically appeals to the attitudes and values of that group, or by (2) disassociating your product from other groups within society, in order to make it appear more accepted, or, in the cases of younger audiences, simply more "cool."

The teenage clothing industry successfully uses both methods, with some advertising directly urging kids to belong to the "youth culture," while other advertising urges them to reject the culture of the "oldies."

For example, in 1969, clothing retailer the Gap flung open its doors in San Francisco, and its very name suggested "generation gap," and that the items inside are unlike those your parents are wearing. Currently with 3,100 stores—including Banana Republic, Old Navy, and

Piperlime—and 2007 revenues of more than $15.8 billion, the associative-dissociative strategy apparently worked.

The bandwagon appeal has worked for scores of companies, including:

* Walgreens: "The pharmacy America trusts."
* Jif Peanut Butter: "Choosy moms choose Jif" (Don't *you* want to be a choosy parent too?)
* Eucerin: "The #1 dermatologist-recommended brand for dry skin."
* British Airways: "The world's favorite airline."
* Glacial Water: "The #1 brand in vended water."
* Mr. Heater: "America's most popular brand of portable heaters."
* Camels: "More doctors smoke Camels than any other cigarette." (Ugh.)
* Rinso: "Who else wants a *whiter* wash—*with no hard work?*"

You can successfully appeal to your prospects' desire to belong in several categories: age, class, sex, geographic, politics, and education, for example. As supported by Cialdini's studies of *comparison cues* (*Influence: Science and Practice*, 1980), by associating your products and services with one or more of these groups, you can successfully persuade an entire category of the public to immediately identify with the attitudes and values of that group, and compel them to purchase your product as a way of showing the world that they now belong to that group. Fascinating, this "psychology stuff," isn't it?

Think. Does your product lend itself to using the *human need to belong* appeal? If it does, don't just think about ways to describe its features and benefits. Put at least equal effort into telling your prospects how buying your product *makes* them (aspirational), *keeps* them (associative), or helps them show the world that they're *not* a part of a particular group (dissociative).

But before your prospects are willing to buy *anything*, they must first be motivated enough to do so! The next technique is based upon one of the classic psychological theories of motivation.

Principle #5: The Means-End Chain—
The Critical Core

"Don't buy my product for what it does for you *today*—buy it for what it *will* do for you *tomorrow!*"

That's what this principle says. And the strategy is based on the theory that many consumer decisions are taken not to satisfy an *immediate* need, but for some *future* objective. For Joe, your buyer, the product, or service he purchased is merely a means to an end.

Luxury goods and services are often advertised using the Means-End Chain. The strategy is to persuade your prospects that your product— although desirable in its own right—will provide additional *secondary* benefits to them or their family.

For example, buying flowers, chocolates, or sexy undergarments as a gift for a partner suggests the possibility of enjoying secondary benefits, doesn't it?

Buying a new car is a wonderful feeling, right? "Forget about that!" Mr. Lexus Salesman tells you. "Because as a realtor, buying that hot new Lexus will make you look more successful to your homebuyers, and they'll be far more likely to list their houses with you. They'll think, 'She must be selling homes...how else could she afford that new Lexus?'"

As the advertiser, your goal is obviously to sell your product or service. Using the Means-End Chain, you simply do it by shifting the consumer's focus to your product's *ultimate* value or benefit. I call it the "benefit of the benefit."

To drive the point home, I ask my CA$HVERTISING seminar audiences, "Why should I buy a window sign for my new retail business? Tell me the *core benefit* of doing so." And here's how the interaction usually goes:

AUDIENCE: "The sign tells people who you are."

ME: "Okay, but what's the *benefit* of telling people who I am?"

AUDIENCE: "So they'll do business with you."

ME: "True, but what's the *benefit* of people doing business with me?"

AUDIENCE: "So you can sell your products, of course!"

ME: "Of course. But what's the *benefit* of me selling my products?"

(And finally, after pulling a few more teeth, someone *finally* shouts...)

AUDIENCE: "So you can make money!"

Hallelujah!

The formula for activating the Means-End Chain mindset is simple. Your copy and images should always represent the positive end results. In this way your prospect is less likely to critically analyze the pros and cons of the actual product, and base their purchase decision on the ultimate benefit it will provide them.

What's the core benefit of your product or service? If you sell shovels, you must understand that people *don't* want a long pole with a flat piece of attached metal. They *do* want the *holes* so they can plant beautiful trees and colorful flowers and make their homes look more attractive!

If you sell microwave ovens, people *don't* want the big, clunky electrical box with all the fancy buttons and the spinning glass plate. They *do* want to be able to cook and eat quickly so they have more time for other things.

Cars? The nice paint, smooth-running engine, and supple leather sure make them fun to drive, but getting from point A to point B is why people really buy them. The ego appeal is icing on the cake.

Just remember, for most products, it's not the product itself that people want, it's the bottom-line *benefit* they're buying. If people could snap their fingers and magically have a hole appear in the ground, you'd be out of the shovel business. If they could cook their food in seconds by wiggling their nose, bye-bye Microwave Warehouse. And chances are if you could teleport yourself from point A to point B like Mr. Spock on *Star Trek*, auto malls and gas stations would be converted into drug stores and condos.

But no matter what you sell, the major difficulty with persuading consumers is dealing with their varying degrees of product knowledge. The following technique uses these differences to its advantage.

Principle #6: The Transtheoretical Model— *Persuasion Step by Step*

If you don't know what a hamburger is, I'm going to have a heck of a time trying to sell you my new "Bloopo Burger," no matter how fresh the beef, fluffy the bun, and tangy the secret sauce may be.

The *Transtheoretical Model* (TTM) divides consumer knowledge and behavior into five stages, and it provides the guidelines for persuading your prospect so they move from complete ignorance of your product ("What the heck is this?"), to making it a regular purchase or an integral part of their lifestyles ("Doesn't everyone buy this?"). When you're aware of these stages, you'll better understand how and where to begin your sales message.

Here are the stages, in a quick and easy nutshell.

* STAGE ONE: *Precontemplation*—People in this stage are either ignorant of your product's existence—"What the heck is a Bloopo Burger?"—or they're unaware they need it.

* STAGE TWO: *Contemplation*—Prospects in this stage *are* aware of your product and have thought about using it. "Hmmm...I should check out those Bloopo Burgers someday."

* STAGE THREE: *Preparation*—This is the planning phase. Your prospect is *thinking* about buying from you, but needs more information about your product's benefits and advantages. "I'd like to buy a Bloopo Burger...it sure looks good, but what the heck is in it? Is it healthier? Better tasting? What's it cost?"

* STAGE FOUR: *Action*—Success! Your prospect has arrived at the coveted *action*, or *purchase* phase. "Here's my credit card, gimme my damned Bloopo!"

* STAGE FIVE: *Maintenance*—A nice place for your prospects to be. In this phase, your product has become part of their everyday lives. They continue to buy your Bloopos without giving it a second thought. It's their burger of choice. Simply put, when they want a burger, they buy a Bloopo.

According to the evidence provided by psychologist James O. Prochaska (1994), the aim for advertisers who use this technique is to move the consumer through the stages one at a time, until using your product becomes a habit. The challenge? Dealing successfully with consumer groups at different stages of the process. Some of your prospects are in stage one, while others wouldn't think of eating any other burger, in stage five. You have two options to tackle this:

1. Create ads that address all five stages. This lets your prospects focus on whatever stage is personally relevant to them. Simply include all the details someone would need to be fully informed about a product they might know little, if anything, about.

2. Create a series of ads that, throughout a period of time, progress from stage one to stage five. Stage one, therefore, introduces your product to the marketplace. Each successive ad builds upon the last, and can begin highlighting key features and benefits.

The objective of both strategies, of course, is to provide your prospects with enough information and motivation to move them through the five stages at their own pace, until they ultimately become regular customers.

No doubt about it. It's far easier to reinforce existing consumer attitudes and behavior than to change those values. The next strategy recognizes this fact and uses it to cement your customers' loyalty.

Principle #7: The Inoculation Theory— *Make Them Prefer You for Life*

When German philosopher Friedrich Nietzsche wrote, "What does not kill me makes me stronger," he could have been talking about this next principle of consumer persuasion.

Inoculation Theory works in much the same way as a vaccination you'd get to prevent the flu. Let me explain. A vaccine consists of a virus that's weakened using a process called *cell culture adaptation*. The virus is grown in chicken embryo cells, which changes the genes that tell the virus how to reproduce. This causes the virus to reproduce poorly in the human body. When injected into your arm, however, your body reacts as if the virus was full strength, and quickly attacks and kills it. In doing so—and this is the important part—*your body actually becomes stronger*, resistant to that specific virus, for the rest of your life.

47

The Inoculation Theory works in a similar way. Developed by social psychologist and Yale professor William J. McGuire, the Inoculation Theory is used to reinforce a consumer's existing attitudes toward a product or service by presenting a "weak" argument that tricks the consumer into defending his position and therefore strengthening his attitude. The three steps are:

1. Warn of an impending attack.
2. Make a weak attack.
3. Encourage a strong defense.

For example, let's say you and I are pastry chefs, and we work together in a bakery turning out the richest, fluffiest, and most amazing chocolate desserts known to man. Your chocolate brand of choice is Guittard, a California-based company whose world-class chocolate is used by many of the most prominent pastry chefs and confectionary shops in the U.S. and abroad. And let's say that I just found out that our boss—Nasty Norman—wants to start using a cheaper (crap) brand.

Since ol' Norm loves to fire employees who disagree with him, I figured that I'd get *you* to fight the chocolate war. Heck, why risk *my* job? The plan: inoculate you. First, according to the strategy, I'd warn you of an impending attack to ready your defenses and get your mind swirling with possible counterattacks. I might say, "Hey, did you hear that Nasty Norm is thinking about buying crappy ChocoWax instead of Guittard to save a few pennies?"

Next, I'd light a fire under you seat with some weak arguments *for* ChocoWax. For example, "Come to think of it, maybe we *could* get away with using ChocoWax by adding a little extra cocoa to our recipes." And, "I wonder if people would really taste the difference. After all, most of our competitors use the el crappo chocolate." (That will *really* fire you up!)

And finally, I'd encourage you to mount a strong defense by getting you to *verbally express* what you're thinking, rather than keeping your thoughts to yourself. "So...what do you think?" Psychological testing shows that the more actively the recipient defends against the attack, the more vigorously he or she will defend the closely held position.

By attacking your ideas and decisions (or brand preferences, as in this example), inoculation encourages you to use critical thought to defend them. Basically, it tricks you into thinking more deeply about your own position, which reinforces your thoughts and feelings. That's because, in an effort to prepare yourself for the impending attack you were warned about in step one ("Norm's going to buy ChocoWax!"), you've begun to plan your counterattack and sharpen your defenses, so when the real attack (from Norm) comes, you'll be prepared to tell him where to put his cheap choc.

Important: Consumer psychologists warn that your attack must be weak. Otherwise you risk having the opposite effect and weakening, or changing your prospects' attitudes. One way advertisers use inoculation is by publicizing their competitors' criticisms of their company, and turning them to their advantage in the form of weak attacks that— thanks to the Inoculation Theory—serve to reinforce and ensure their consumers' loyalty.

Inoculation is a favorite among politicians. Their stock line goes this way: *"My opponent will tell you* there's no way to bring down skyrocketing oil prices...*he'll tell you* that the only way to balance the national budget is to raise your taxes...*he'll tell you* that it's good enough to provide health insurance for most citizens, not all of them. But I tell you this is definitely not the case, and here is why...."

Do you see what's happening? This candidate is inoculating his audience by (1) warning them of an impending attack, (2) presenting the weak arguments his opponent will say during the campaign, and (3) encouraging a strong defense by giving them a little ammunition to help prepare for battle.

An auto body shop might take aim at the competition by adopting a consumer-advocate-type position by telling prospects to be wary when getting quotes from competitors: *"Our competitors will tell you* that the little dent in your fender costs over $1,000 to fix. *They'll quote you* $800 to replace your windshield because of that tiny chip in the glass. What they won't tell you is there are many 'insider' secrets in our business for getting these jobs done for a fraction of the cost. For example...."

So how can you quash your competitors' sales arguments by launching a preemptive strike using the Inoculation Theory? The key is to prep them in such a way so that your prospects process your competitors' claims though *your* filters! Like the auto body shop owner in the last example, tell them what to look out for; what's good; what's bad; what's suspect. Doing so implies that you're so confident in what *you* sell that you're inviting closer inspection. You *want* them to compare!

And I don't use the term *consumer advocate* lightly. The fact is, if you're providing legitimate information—and I trust you are—then your advertising becomes more than just another business shouting "Me! Me! Me! Buy from ME!" You're actually providing a helpful service that—assuming your product or service is truly better—will translate into additional business and tremendous public goodwill.

Are you a pizza shop? *"Our competitors tell you* they use fresh mozzarella, *but they don't tell you* they buy it pre-shredded in big plastic bags. At Pauley's Pizza, we hand-shred our mozzarella every morning. Our competitors offer you a choice of thin and crispy or deep dish Sicilian, *but they don't tell you* that they buy their dough in hard frozen balls and thaw it out the night before. At Pauley's Pizza, we make our dough fresh every single day. *Our competitors tell you* how convenient their home delivery service is, *but they don't tell you* that their average delivery time is over an hour. Pauley's Pizza delivers in 28 minutes or your pizza is free."

Ads similar to these create more critical consumers that are predisposed to your products. This "Ralph Nadar approach" builds great trust and credibility. Take a real hard look at what you're selling. What do you do better, faster, easier? Inoculate your prospects by bringing these advantages to light and watch how you'll win them over.

Principle #8: Belief Re-ranking—
Change Their Reality

Let's face it: Most people don't like change. As impervious as bullfrogs are to water, human beings are to doing things differently. It's tough enough to get people to change small physical things about themselves: the way they dress, their hairstyle, the way they work, the way they speak. Trying to get them to change their beliefs about life? Ugh! You see, psychologists know that even if our beliefs are inaccurate or inconsistent—even if *we ourselves* know they are—we'll still defend them as if their existence is somehow linked to our very survival! Link anything to survival—and that's exactly what the ego does, by the way—and you're up against a brutally tough opponent.

Fortunately, there *are* ways to change people's beliefs about your product, the primary belief being that *they don't want or need it!* One of the most effective of these methods works by switching the focus away from the attitudes themselves and onto the underlying beliefs.

Change the Focus of the Beliefs

In order to influence beliefs, advertisers use images and statistics that appeal either to emotions, such as fear, humor, or guilt (affecting the right-hemisphere, creative brain), or to the consumer's intellect, through factual evidence and examples (affecting the left-hemisphere, logical brain). When you do this, you present your audience with an alternative view of reality—one that's not supported by their currently held beliefs. In other words, you might feel a certain way about a product, but your beliefs can be changed if you're given new ways to think about it.

The Baking Soda Blues

For example, let's say you love baking soda toothpaste because you read somewhere that it's the easiest—and least expensive—way to whiten your teeth at home. In fact, you've told all your friends and family that they too should be using baking soda toothpaste if they want super-white choppers. "Baking soda, baking soda, baking soda." You won't shut the heck up about the damned baking soda. You've been using the toothpaste for more than a decade. And you've recommended it *so* much that your friends and family are afraid to smile in front of you for fear of being chastised should their teeth not meet your annoying new dental-whiteness standards.

One day, however, you see a disturbing article in the newspaper. Oh no! A quote about baking soda by Ken Burrell, D.D.S., senior director of the American Dental Association Council on Scientific Affairs, sends you reeling: "We think the public believes there is some benefit, but in fact, there is no evidence to show any therapeutic value."

Horrors! "How can this possibly be?!" you shout. Mental storm clouds roll in, lightning strikes, and the first chink in your enamel-white armor appears.

But it doesn't stop there. Shortly thereafter you read this quote from *another* respected dentist, "Baking soda has a taste sensation that makes teeth feel good, but there is no proven therapeutic value."

Gulp. Before you know it, you're standing in front of the mirror examining the whiteness of your teeth, wondering if all that white sparkle was simply a pigment of your imagination. Your own dentist confirms the horrible truth, and your baking soda sandcastle comes crumbling down. Your feelings were attacked by reason, and eventually, critical thinking—via central route processing—emerged the victor.

The Kung Fu Concession

Let's say you really dislike any form of violence, but you're not comfortable walking the streets anymore because of the recent surge in violent crimes in your area. Your friends are taking Wing Chun Kung Fu—a lightning-fast and practical style for self defense—but you're not interested. "And that's that!" you say. Well, one day a friend hands you a brochure from her Wing Chun school. It's filled with gruesome stats about local-area crime rates. And it contains testimonials from current students who describe how they successfully defended themselves against attackers. They talk about how safe the training is, how easy it was to learn, how patient and caring the instructors are. The next day, another friend whose child takes lessons tells you how her child defended herself against the schoolyard bully. Like sprinkling radish seeds on fertile soil, new thoughts start to grow.

Fast forward to one week later. Walking in a dark parking lot back to your car you think you're being followed! Luckily it's a false alarm. But it happens again another night. And then every 10th person looks suspicious. And suddenly all you're doing is thinking about those crime stats, that Kung Fu brochure with the success stories you keep reading, and how your friends and their children successfully used what they've learned. And before you know it, you're watching your friend in class, and you're now one step closer to becoming the school's newest member.

Of course, your prospects may remain suspicious of the ideas you present, and many will reject the ad—just as they can with any other ad. (A 100-percent response rate is still the stuff of advertisers' dreams.) But many others will amend their beliefs in order to harmoniously exist with their new perceptions. Not to do so causes *cognitive dissonance*, an uncomfortable feeling that happens when you simultaneously hold conflicting thoughts or beliefs—something the human mind dislikes intensely.

Change the Importance of the Beliefs

Another approach is to change the *importance* of beliefs, rather than the beliefs themselves. That's because it's easier to strengthen or weaken an existing belief than it is to change it.

The most successful method is to strengthen your prospects' current beliefs either by supporting them with factual evidence (pouring on the stats, reports, studies, testimonials), or by using everyday examples (success stories from other users, for example) with which your prospects can identify. Many advertisers take this technique one step further and reinforce *additional* beliefs, which are unlikely to meet with resistance because they don't conflict with existing beliefs.

The strategy of manipulating current beliefs, either through *reinforcement* or *undermining*, is far easier and more likely to succeed than attempting a wholesale change of basic beliefs. That's why it's the more popular persuasion strategy.

For example, nowadays everyone knows that smoking and excessive drinking are not good for your health. But no matter how often or how forcefully you stress these points, consumers' defensive tachometers redline instantly if they sense that they're being criticized or attacked. "You talkin' to me? You talkin' to *me?*"

How do you avoid this? By either (1) reinforcing the beliefs of those prospects who already hold a positive view about your product, or (2) by subtly offering an alternative set of beliefs to those you wish to convert.

For example, advertisers of food and drink know that most consumers today believe in the importance of a healthy, balanced diet. They can reinforce this belief—and gain an advantage over their rivals—by emphasizing that *their* brand contains vitamin x, y, or z, or is sugar free, or any other health-related benefit that will build upon the audience's currently held beliefs. (Simply put, we're adding on to what we know they already believe. We're giving them more of what we know they want to hear: how healthy our product is for them.)

Remember: we don't want to cause any negative reactions. Our goal is not to fight with our prospects. We don't want to tell them they're wrong. We want to change their beliefs without causing a negative, defensive reaction.

For instance, rather than blatantly stating "Milk is healthier than soda," you should present images and factual examples of the potential health risks posed by soda, and compare that with equally graphic and persuasive evidence for the health benefits of milk. See the difference? This way, you avoid a head-on collision with your prospects' existing beliefs. You weasel your way in, so to speak.

Now listen carefully. Regardless of what technique you use, your prospects must remain unaware that you're attempting to influence them. You want them to think they've made their own decision. This way there are no bruised egos; they claim the decision as their own, and it's far more likely to become cemented in future new behavior.

"Gotcha, Drew...but how do I do this?"

You do it by removing your prospects' need for cognitive (critical) thinking. The following technique makes it easier for you by dividing products into those that require a lot of cognitive thought, and those that require little.

Principle #9: The Elaboration Likelihood Model—*Adjust Their Attitude*

It's quite a mouthful, isn't it? Don't fret. We touched on this earlier, so now let's dig in! The Elaboration Likelihood Model, or ELM, suggests there are two routes to attitude change: the *central route* and the *peripheral route*. Here's the difference:

* The central route: Persuading using logic, reasoning, and deep thinking.
* The peripheral route: Persuading using the association of pleasant thoughts and positive images, or "cues."

Which method should *you* use? That depends on your product. The *peripheral route* encourages consumers to consciously—or often unconsciously—focus on superficial images and "cues" in order to influence attitudes and decisions, without any serious consideration of the ad's content.

By contrast, the *central route* encourages your audience to really think about it...to consider the ad's issues and arguments before reaching any decision, especially making a purchase.

The ELM Rule of Thumb

You think harder, longer, and deeper about important purchases than you do for unimportant ones, right? Of course. Psychologists say that consumers' motivation tends to be higher when they're considering products with "high personal relevance." That's fancy talk for something that either costs big bucks, or is important (to the buyer) in some way—such as earthquake insurance for someone whose house teeters precipitously on the San Andreas fault (for example, uh, like mine).

You're not going to purchase a $928,000 house using the same thought process that you'd use to buy a can of pork and beans, right? Of course not. The two buying decisions require different levels, qualities, and depths of thought. When thinking about buying the house, your brain switches to central route processing. Meaning that you'll carefully consider all the arguments and analyze all available facts. "Let's see...interest rates on the 5-year adjustable rate mortgage compare favorably to 30-year fixed...our current debt-to-income ratio is 18 percent...and if we put down at least 20 percent we won't need to pay for private mortgage insurance, thereby lowering our monthly payments."

That's an example of left-brain thinking, referring to the side of your brain that controls logical thought and reasoning; crunching numbers and weighing options. And it's the kind of thinking you *ought* to do before making such a purchase. Buy the wrong house and—after uprooting your family, moving across the country away from family and friends, and starting a new job—you could easily wind up shackled in a self-created financial and emotional torture chamber.

By contrast, when you're holding two cans of baked beans, your brain presses the big peripheral route button, and the result is simply, "Yum. Beans!" No big decision here. And not much brain power is needed. After all, if you buy the wrong beans, you simply say, "Blorf...lousy beans!" and dump them down the drain.

So what kind of thought process does purchasing *your* product require?

If Your Product Requires:	Then Do This:
Central Route Processing	Pour on the facts, stats, evidence, testimonials, studies, reports, and case histories. Weave them into your most persuasive sales argument.
Peripheral Route Processing	Load your ads full of colorful, pleasant images, humorous or popular subject matter, or the sponsorship of celebrities.

When advertising your peripheral route product, don't neglect including the features and benefits, of course. Just realize that most consumers won't rack their brains over which brand of sugar, paperclips, or thimbles to buy. These things—and many others—are simply not "deep thought" purchases and therefore don't require deep-thought ad content.

Don't get me wrong. I didn't say you don't need to do anything but show some smiling faces and a photo of my cute flat-coated retriever Joey to rake in sales. You should still give basic data to satisfy their fundamental data needs. If you sell ink-jet paper, for example, you still want to state its size, color, weight, sheet quantity, and even the TAPPI Brightness Standard rating. If you have competitors—and most of us do—and your product is better than theirs in some way, for heaven's sake, *say it!*

Cues Feel Good, But Central Route Processing Makes Them Prefer You

Yesterday they couldn't get enough of your product. Today they can't even remember its name. Why? The Elaboration Likelihood Model provides an explanation for why some attitudes persist throughout a consumer's lifetime, whereas others are less stable and more prone to change. Research has found that attitudes based on central route processing are more resistant to counter-persuasion, and show greater attitude-behavior consistency than attitudes formed by peripheral route thinking.

It makes perfect sense. Because when you use central route processing, you support your decisions with well-considered mental arguments that you're constantly seeking to reinforce and strengthen. "After all," you say, "I gave it a lot of thought...I know it was the right decision." (Notice how attitudes formed by central route processing become so closely aligned with the ego that they become inseparable. Anyone who challenges something you carefully thought about—put a lot of "think time" into—seems to be challenging your very intelligence!)

Want examples? *Look around you!* Talk to people about any topic in which they spent a ridiculous amount of time in mental exploration, reinforcement, and justification: religion, politics, abortion, child-rearing, and education, for examples. Their positions on topics such as these are stubbornly persistent and tenaciously resistant to change.

Now ask these same people, "What kind of soap do you use? What brands of cereal do you eat?" For products such as these, and others, they may have preferences, but their attitudes about them can typically be easily changed.

One last thing you should know about the ELM. Attitudes developed using central route processing will last longer than those formed by the peripheral route. Simply put, logic and reason burn themselves into the brain far more deeply than good feelings created by visual cues or other emotion-stimulating catalysts.

Remember: When you get someone to think deeply about something, and you persuade them to arrive at a conclusion, they will adopt their decision as a result of their own thinking, protect it, and defend it against (competitors') attacks as if it were their "baby"—their "brainchild."

By using the peripheral route to persuasion, advertisers are relying on the effectiveness of what social psychologists call *cues*, as we discussed earlier. These cues are mental shortcuts that, if utilized correctly, can convey an ad's message without the need to engage the consumer in any form of deep thought. The following technique is based upon the influence that can be exerted by using the right cue for the right occasion.

Principle #10: The 6 Weapons of Influence—*Shortcuts to Persuasion*

Social psychologist Robert Cialdini is a clever guy. In preparing his book *Influence: The Psychology of Persuasion* (1998), he took three years and went undercover performing a variety of jobs to watch influence in action. Posing as everything from a used car salesman to a telemarketer, he studied the words and behaviors that move people to comply...and *buy*. From this, he developed his Cues of Life model that describes how people are persuaded using six general "Cues of Influence."

These cues are mental shortcuts, and are effective in many different situations—especially when your prospect isn't using careful, "considered" thought. Use these cues when you're writing an ad using the peripheral route to persuasion, but *fuhgeddaboutit* if buying your product requires lots of thought, reasoning, and maybe even a little justification, such as a luxury item or a high-cost *anything* at all.

Known by the mnemonic CLARCCS, Cialdini's six cues are:

1. Comparison: The power of your peers.
2. Liking: The Balance Theory. "I like you...*take my money!*"
3. Authority: Cracking the code of credibility.
4. Reciprocation: What goes around comes around...*profitably!*
5. Commitment/consistency: The "Four Walls" technique.
6. Scarcity: Get 'em while they last!

- -

Cue #1: Comparison

Let's first look at comparison, which is similar to group persuasion—or the bandwagon effect—and is an extremely potent weapon in your advertising armory. The question, "Everybody else is doing it, why aren't you?" exerts a powerful effect on consumers. Human psychology teaches us that no one likes to be left out, and that we're all driven by a need to belong (See Principle #4: The Bandwagon Effect). Therefore, if someone sees his or her friends, family, or peers wearing a certain fashion (low-cut sneaker socks, for example, putting a certain bumper sticker on their car ("Support Our Troops!"), or drinking a specific brand of beer (Corona with a juicy lime wedge), there's enormous pressure to conform, both *internal* ("Gee...everyone's wearing really short sneaker socks...mine are really high; I wonder if I look like a dork.") and external ("Hey Drew, what's with the dorky high white socks? You look like that geek from our 1977 gym class!").

As an advertiser, this is a godsend. Because if I can successfully convey the message that my product is the one that a certain group should choose, then my sales could snowball simply from creating this mindset.

Cue #2: Liking

Liking says, in effect, "Because you like me, you should do as I say: BUY!" This potent cue applies whenever a consumer feels a connection with a representative of a company, the characters or personalities in an ad, or another user of the product.

For example, I used to work with a woman named Dianne. She used to sell everything from candles to baskets. And she'd always pass around her catalogs to other employees and ask for orders. I watched many succumb to the pressure of the *liking* cue. She had the kind of personality that made you instantly like her. But what about the quality of the candles and baskets she sold? Oh, that didn't matter one bit. Because it was the internal pressure to accommodate or please Dianne—driven by the *liking* cue—that caused so many people to buy from her.

Similarly, when a coworker you like storms into your office and says, "Hey...my daughter Ariel is doing a fund raiser for cancer research...would you please sponsor her in his race?" Wow...talk about a triple whammy! (1) Daughter, (2) cancer, and (3) the person asking. You're screwed. Just sign the form and fork over the cash.

Remember: The lynchpin of the sale is *liking*—you must *like* the person for it to work. And this liking could be focused on anyone involved in the transaction, whether it's the person handing out flyers on the street corner, the celebrity whose face adorns an ad, or the friend who purchased the same brand last week and is now urging you to do likewise.

The Better They Look, the More Others Like

"Don't judge a book by its cover" is a great expression, but that's *exactly* what people do when they look into the eyes of a person they consider attractive. Many psychological and sociological experiments have concluded that attractive people exert a greater influence on others, and are considered to be more trustworthy and likable (Down & Lyons, *Personality and Social Psychology Bulletin*, 1991). No wonder most ads feature happy, attractive faces smiling out at the consumer from the pages of magazines, newspapers, and direct mail catalogs.

And here's another interesting fact: Contrary to popular belief, men are most attracted to pictures of other men, and women to pictures of other *women*. Why? Psychologists say: *Identification*. All of us are interested primarily in ourselves; no one is more important to you than you. When an ad shows a picture of a handsome, important-looking man, for example, other men will identify with that person, step into his shoes, and briefly become handsome and important-looking themselves. This same principle applies to women.

Cue #3: Authority

The third cue is authority, and it's a mental shortcut used since the beginning of time. Many healthcare products have long relied on the endorsement of the "man in the white coat" for authority. Just as people trust the word of their doctor, dentist, or optician, they'll generally accept the authority of any official-looking person who endorses an advertised product.

This is a prime example of the peripheral route to persuasion in action. Using an official, intelligent, or authoritative figure to promote a product saves consumers the trouble of researching or examining the issues, and they simply accept the facts and claims as being true. In fact, before the FCC cracked down on it, many advertisers hired actors who played doctors in popular TV shows to endorse their aspirin, cold remedies and other medical-related products, fully outfitted in the doctor

59

costumes they wore in the shows. Funny, isn't it? The viewers *knew* these people were just actors, yet they were still persuaded by the powerful authority cue built by their characters. The cue is so powerful that it didn't even matter when the FCC forced these actors to say "I'm not really a doctor, but I play one on TV...." They still bought!

Think! What authority in *your* industry does your target market respect? Do whatever you can to get a testimonial or full-blown endorsement. Then get permission to use this person's image in your marketing. Pay the authority to do a short video you can use on your Website or on a DVD. Then add a list of persuasive facts, figures, and scientific-looking graphs, and the authority cue can help you make a lot of money.

Cue #4: Reciprocation

During a CA$HVERTISING workshop, I asked someone in my audience, "Eileen, are you well-mannered?" She quickly shot back, "Of course I am!" I continued, "Okay, then what do you do when someone gives you something?" She says, "I say 'thank you.'" I continue, "Yes...and then what do you feel compelled to do?" She thinks a moment and blurts out, *"Uh...give them something in return?"* Exactly!

This is the basis of the mental cue known as reciprocation, and it's a favorite of catalog companies, subscription magazines, and any business engaged in sampling. Did you ever wonder how these companies could afford to give away freebies with every first order? The reason is *reciprocation*. They give you something, and you're compelled to purchase something from them in return. The influence is so strong, in fact, that the free gift may be nothing more than a scratchy 2-cent pen filled with only a week's worth of ink.

Why does it work? Because the company has given you something, and you accepted it! Social convention now decrees that you're obligated to give something back. It's why survey companies often send you a one-dollar bill to thank you for completing the survey. The four-page survey may contain 100 tedious questions, but the dollar makes you feel that you *should* do it. It's fascinating.

Here's another familiar example. Walk through many major U.S. airports and you might be handed a rose by a member of the Hare Krishna religious group. Upon accepting this free gift, you're then asked to make a donation. Because you already accepted the gift, you're compelled to comply. You'd feel badly if you didn't. Ahhh...there's that childhood training again, and it's now a programmed response. At least now you're aware of it, and now you can use it to your advantage.

Jay Siff, a wonderful client of many years, uses the reciprocation principle to the hilt. His company, Moving Targets of Perkasie, Pennsylvania (MovingTargets.com), sends gift certificates to people who just moved into the neighborhood on behalf of his primarily restaurant and auto-shop clients. Free pizza, free entrée, free oil change. Not only does the service introduce new movers to the retailers' businesses, but it also sets the reciprocation ball in motion. When they're done chomping on that pizza, or driving away with a fresh oil fill—assuming they were both treated right and satisfied—not only do they have good feelings about the business, but they're also far more likely to return and spend money, often becoming loyal long-term customers. Moving Target's use of the reciprocation principle is so refined and effective—and has been for more than 16 years—that many companies use it as their primary marketing strategy.

What can *you* give away to start the reciprocation ball rolling? I'm not talking about some junky little trinket, like a cheap key ring featuring your logo and phone number. You want to give something of value. Something that makes your recipient think, "Hey, wow, wasn't that thoughtful?" Can you give a free sample? A gift certificate? If you're a consultant, how about giving 30 minutes of your time with no obligation? Many attorneys offer free first consultations, but that's not what I'm talking about here. The reciprocation mindset is initiated when you give something to someone as a gift. It's not something they should have to *request* from you. (If I have to request it, it's a *favor*.) And it's not something you give me in return for something I've done. (That's a *thank you*.)

Here are some examples of what I'm talking about.

* Are you a dog groomer? Give a free flea and tick collar.
* Are you a bakery? Give a free rye bread or a box of chocolate chip cookies.
* Are you a bike shop? Give a free water bottle.
* Are you an old-fashioned shoe repair shop? Give a free shine.
* Are you a karate school? Give a month of free lessons.
* Are you a printer? Give 50 free photocopies.
* Are you a florist? Give a free bunch of flowers.

* Are you a cigar shop? Give a free lighter.
* Are you a pizzeria? Give a free slice.

Whoever you are, give away *something*...and let the magic of reciprocation turn mere prospects into profitable, perhaps long-term customers.

Cue #5: *Commitment/Consistency*

In Disney's popular *Haunted Mansion*, an eerie voice threatens, "Look around you. Your logic cannot deny that this chamber has no windows and no doors. Which offers a rather logical challenge...to find...a way...out." (Cue demonic laughter.)

That's the object of the commitment/consistency cue, also known as the "Four Walls" technique—not to scare buyers away, but to box them in, cause them to take a stand, and make a request that would demonstrate their commitment to their stand. You create an ad that poses four questions to your prospect, with each answer leading logically to the next, until, at the end of your ad, your prospect is all but committed to making the purchase (Cialdini, 1980).

The commitment/consistency cue says that if you take a stand on an issue, you *must remain consistent with your beliefs*. This is a powerful psychological tactic, and one that's more effective when used in person, because the cue relies on social pressure as its engine. For example, someone knocks on your door and says, "Hi! Would you please sign my petition to help reduce neighborhood crime and make our streets safer?" No-brainer, right? So you sign away. Now that you've committed to that very reasonable stance, society expects you to remain consistent with it. *And so you will*. That's why when the petitioner next says, "Great! Thank you. And now would you please make a small tax-deductible $3 donation because we need to buy two-way radios for the neighborhood watch?" Yikes. You've been boxed in, my friend. And now you can do little else but gulp, reach into your pocket, and hand over the cash. You were a lab rat in an experiment, and you behaved exactly as anticipated. To *not* donate the $3 is infinitely more difficult than if (1) you didn't support the cause (you'd have no reason to donate), or (2) you weren't *first* asked to sign the petition. Because you did, however, the petitioner had already pre-closed you, and the natural next step was to simply extract your moolah. The closing question—whatever it is—says, in effect, "Okay, you've declared your stance. Let's see if you're now going to support your own declared position." To not do so is the ultimate in hypocrisy.

Although not as effective in print as in person, here's how the principle looks on paper. You'd start by asking questions that stimulate the response you're seeking:

Are you afraid to walk the streets alone? Don't you wish there was an easy way to protect yourself against muggers and other low-life scum who prey on innocent people? You know the ones I mean: The dirt bags who step right into your face and ask—threateningly—"you got some spare change?" Wouldn't it be great if there was a safe, effective, and easy way to stop thugs cold at the push of a button? A way that gives you instant and total control over even the most savage 350-pound, drug-blitzed maniac who has the gall to try to intimidate—and possibly terribly injure—you and your family? Introducing *The Tesla Sizzler*...the world's first personal anti-mugging microwave force field....

The idea is to elicit a string of "yes" responses from your prospect, each successive answer adding momentum, creating a snowball of interest and desire, and presenting your product as the path to fulfillment. Because there's no human interaction, there's also no social pressure for you to be consistent with your answers, meaning to buy. Just because you're interested in preventing getting mugged and you find the whole idea of cooking local muggers with personal microwave guns fascinating, there's no one interacting with you to escort you to the next step in the sales process. Without this social pressure, the ad relies on a multitude of copy and design techniques to encourage you to read the whole sales pitch and then pick up the phone and place your order. Effectively written long-copy direct-response ads do exactly this.

Cue #6: *Scarcity*

The last of Cialdini's cues is *scarcity*. If, in addition to telling you all the benefits of attending, I say, "My CA$HVERTISING workshop has very limited seating and is very difficult to buy tickets for," then it becomes more desirable. Why? Simply, we want what we cannot have.

Take the Cabbage Patch Kids craze of 1983. People went bonkers trying to buy these ugly vinyl-faced dolls. They knocked over display tables, screamed, cursed, and fought like rabid cats in department stores. One particularly unruly crowd of 1,000 would-be Cabbage Patch "parents" turned violent after waiting eight hours and stormed a Zayre store in Wilkes-Barre, Pennsylvania. Wielding a baseball bat, the manager kept the frenzied buyers at bay. The fact is, the success of these dolls caught the Coleco company off guard: they couldn't produce enough to satisfy demand. In fact, the consumer affairs department of New York's Nassau County filed a lawsuit accusing Coleco of "harassing" children by advertising dolls that weren't available, forcing the company to suspend advertising. Too funny. And too late. The scarcity effect had already thrust its hooks into the American doll-buying consciousness, and that, in turn, fueled even *greater* demand.

If you can't have it, you suddenly want it. It's like the armrest you weren't using in the movie theater or airplane. As soon as someone sits beside you and starts using it, you suddenly have a strong desire to somehow "get it back." You feel as if they took "your" armrest. And it might continue to annoy you the entire length of the movie or until your flight lands. Hmmm...when you *had* it, you didn't want it. When someone took it from you, there was nothing you wanted more. Interesting how we humans are wired.

The most common manifestation of the scarcity principle is the use of lines such as *one-day sale*, *limited offer*, *only while supplies last*, or *first come, first served*, all which make the product appear in short supply, and therefore increases consumer interest. The success of this technique is apparent—every business uses it! Using the scarcity cue is like using a deadline, except scarcity also suggests exclusivity, not simply limited supply. Ahhh...now that's a powerful one-two punch if I ever saw one.

In a twist of the scarcity cue, I've seen several business consultants announce, "Steve is finally available to accept three more clients. But hurry! Because once his roster is full, his services won't be available for another two years." In this example, consultant Steve is emphasizing scarcity by telling you he's now available...with an added zinger that warns you that you better act fast.

Principle #11: Message Organization— *Attaining Critical Clarity*

Understand if you saying don't what I'm, persuade I can't you. *Huh?* The point is clear. "If you don't understand what I'm saying, I can't persuade you." Even if you have the greatest product in the world, the slickest-looking sales materials, and scores of hot testimonials from customers who light candles for you every night, if your ads are disorganized or poorly structured, your cash register ain't gonna ring! Even worse, you could actually *harm* your business with ads that leave your prospects with an inaccurate or totally incorrect interpretation of your intended message—something that could negatively affect you for a long time.

That's why ad agencies and the psychologists they employ are careful to ensure that, whatever the strength of the message, it must always be well organized and easily and accurately understood. Simple is better, but simple isn't necessarily *easy*. Communicating clearly and plainly takes practice. But fret not. I devote an entire technique to this topic in the next chapter, in "Ad Agency Secret #1: The Psychology of Simplicity." After reading it, you'll know exactly what to do and how to do it.

Principle #12: Examples vs. Statistics— *And the Winner Is...*

Which is more persuasive: examples or statistics? Read the following two paragraphs and decide.

EXAMPLE

It's a motor car like none other, with a gracious, parlor-like cabin that beckons your entrance. Accept its invitation...swing closed its vault-like door...and prepare yourself for a driving experience reserved only for a privileged few. Surrounded by rich, fragrant leathers, exotic hardwoods, and costly Wilton wool carpeting, this vehicle spotlights your discriminating lifestyle...your insistence on the finest. Now turn the key and the world's most refined automotive power plant instantly awakens. Shift into drive...accelerate...and thrill to a rush surpassing the descriptive capacity of words alone. *Feel it?* That's adrenaline coursing through your veins, as 453 muscular horses beckon you to set them free....

STATISTICS

* 6,749 cc 6.7 liters V 12 front engine with 92.0 mm bore, 84.6 mm stroke, 11.0 compression ratio, variable valve timing/camshaft and four valves per cylinder.

* Power: 338 kW, 453 HP SAE @ 5,350 rpm; 531 ft lb, 720 Nm @ 3,500 rpm.

* External dimensions: overall length (inches): 202.8, overall width (inches): 78.2, overall height (inches): 62.2, wheelbase (inches): 130.7, front track (inches): 66.4, rear track (inches): 65.8 and curb to curb turning circle (feet): 43.0.

* Luxury trim wood and leather on doors, and wood and leather on dashboard.

Which of these—example or statistics—is more appealing to you? Which whets your appetite for more? Most importantly, *which really sells you?* If you're like most people, the example did the trick. Sure, the stats are nice to know, but when it comes to making the cash register go *ka-ching*, you should always place your money on the example. Why? In a word: *emotion*, the key to sales.

The example you just read—and the emotion it elicits—puts you smack behind the wheel of a brand new, $403,000 Rolls Royce Phantom ultra-luxury "saloon" automobile. And did you notice what happened when you read it? I caused you to test drive—to demonstrate—the product inside your head! In fact, no matter what you sell—even a $10 mouse trap—until you can get your prospects to imagine themselves *using* your product or service, they're not going to take the next step and *buy* it. Featuring colorful examples causes what I call "self-demonstration," and boosts your prospects' desire to own and motivation to buy.

In addition, research has shown that well-written examples, (1) relate more closely consumer's personal experiences, and (2) are easier to comprehend because they require less mental effort to process (Petty & Cacioppo, 1986). No wonder most ads and TV commercials use testimonials and endorsements rather than long lists of facts and figures. They're simply more dramatic and engaging.

"But Drew! Some people *do* want to know facts and figures!" Of course they do. And depending upon what kind of product you're selling, you *should* include them. But not to the exclusion of strong, emotionally provoking examples. And a good case can be made for including both examples *and* statistics in your ads. The proportion of each should be carefully considered so you don't alienate either group. "But how do I know that?" Simple: Your product will tell you.

* **Do you sell beer?** Forget the stats. Show attractive people, barely dressed hardbodies, and good times.

* **Cars?** Play up the examples and include some stats for the performance, safety, or efficiency enthusiasts, whichever category of buyer to whom your particular model appeals.

* **Laser printers?** This is primarily a utilitarian product, isn't it? So tell how much paper it holds, how fine its resolution, how long the ink lasts, its maximum monthly duty cycle, and other relevant stats. No one gets turned on thinking about ink jets. (At least none that I know, and many of my friends are professional writers!)

* **Landscape services?** Your product is all about beauty, self-image (how your property looks to the neighbors), and convenience (never having to mow your lawn on those hot, sweaty summer days). Plenty of opportunity for examples here!

* **Gym memberships?** Pure emotion here. Show photos of lean and attractive men and women, before and after shots, and testimonials from happy members. Sure, you can say how many exercise machines you have and the square footage of your facility, but it's those photos that'll hook 'em.

Principle #13: Message Sidedness — *Dual-Role Persuasion*

There are two sides to every story, right? Well, the same is true in advertising. You can present just *your* side of the story...or you can present your side *and* your competitor's side in a head-to-head product comparison.

Although one-sided messages are simpler (because you're discussing only your product), studies show that two-sided messages are more persuasive, but only if they stick to the format of defending their own position while also attacking the competition (Allen, 1991).

The key is to present both sides and still advocate only one—*your own*. How? By making your two-sided message *appear* to the reader as fair-minded and balanced. For example:

Acme makes an excellent fly swatter, and they've been doing so for years. Heck, in the 1940s and '50s they were the most popular way to kill the pesky critters. And they did a darn good job back then. However, now it's the 21st century. And it's time to step up to full-scale fly-swatting automation, with our new *RoboSwat Laser-Powered Anti-Fly Gun Turret.* So easy and effective, it makes old-fashioned (and messy) swatters obsolete!

Using the peripheral route to persuasion (superficial thinking, remember?), your audience is likely to think that your two-sided message is more thoughtful and credible than your competition's one-sided ads that talk only about themselves. Complimenting the other company on its fine products instantly makes your prospect think, "Hmmm...they're being fair to the other firm, not bashing them, actually saying nice things, but simply pointing out that theirs is better." If your prospect decides to use central processing (deep thinking and reasoning) and considers the message carefully, the combination of defense and attack makes them think even more systematically about the issue, and start questioning the validity of the other side. So not only does it help persuade prospects to favor your product, but it also helps turn them against those of your rivals.

Comparison ads don't have to be about bashing the other guy into submission. You can calmly point out the advantages your product provides. What benefits do you offer that they don't? Is yours faster? Easier? Cleaner? Healthier? More fun? Less expensive? More effective? Comparison charts that point out your product's advantages at a glance are extremely effective. Consumers interpret such charts as, "Ahhh...all the research has been done for me. All I need to do now is buy." This is peripheral processing at its best. That's because a central-route thinker would say, "Hmm...sounds good, but how do I know these facts are right? I'm going to check what the other company is saying. After all, these people are trying to persuade me to buy!" The fact is, however, most people are lazy peripheral-route thinkers, and the comparison chart is all they need to make their buying decision. So be a good sport. Tell both sides. Compliment what's good about your competition. It might even make you feel good. Then say why *you're* even better. The persuasive impact resulting in additional sales will definitely make you feel great!

You can even play both sides yourself. You'll recall back in the Preface I said if you're afraid of the words *persuasion* and *influence* you should "stop reading" because "this book is not for you." I was playing take-away, telling you that you couldn't have something in an effort to make you want it even more. Don't ever be afraid to tell people why they *shouldn't* buy what you're selling. Not only does it boost your credibility, but if they're true prospects, it'll also add fire to their desire.

Principle #14: Repetition and Redundancy—*The Familiarity Factor*

"People don't start seeing your ad until you run it seven times."

Did you ever hear that one? It's likely based on a similar expression used in personal selling: "It takes an average of seven sales calls to close a deal." Whatever the actual number is, repetition is an important factor in getting your point across in advertising. Repeating your message not only helps break down walls of disinterest, but with each repetition your ad also gets exposed to those who may not have noticed it the last time.

What's more, with each repetition of your message, your audience naturally grows more familiar with your product and company. And unless they have some reason to think otherwise, a feeling of acceptance begins to grow. As this acceptance strengthens, an affinity begins to develop. They, in essence, begin to feel comfortable with you. This comfort leads to greater trust, which opens the door to the sale.

Remember: The aim of all advertising is *to create marginal differences in consumer attitudes and perceptions*. Through repetition, these small differences can build into larger differences, and can often tip the balance in favor of the advertised brand.

Can repetition be bad? Possibly. Research suggests that there's an optimum level at which repetition is effective, but that beyond this level it can lead to frustration and consumer "turn-off" (Petty and Cacioppo, 1979). In short, the study involved presenting arguments to college students about increasing university spending. Some students heard the argument once, others three times, the rest five times. Student who were exposed to three repetitions backed the spending proposition. In the students who heard it five times, agreement dropped off considerably. Researchers Petty and Cacioppo suggested that at this high level of frequency, tedium may have set in, which caused the student to attack what they then considered to be an offensive communication.

Please don't construe this to mean that you shouldn't run your ads more frequently than three times! Asking college kids about university spending isn't the same as advertising your products and services in your local newspaper. I shared this example simply to make you aware that endless repetition isn't necessary a good thing, and to caution you to be sensitive to its use. Hey, just because *you* love your ad doesn't mean your audience will. But if it's making you money, by all means, keep it humming. Use repetition wisely and you'll build brand familiarity. Overuse it, and you could be growing a bumper crop of consumer contempt.

Run the same ad over and over, and you're being repetitious. Run different variations of the same ad, and you're taking advantage of the power of *redundancy*. This is a simple way to extend the life span of an effective message or slogan. By presenting the same message in a different format and slightly different copy, you trick the reader into believing he's seeing a new ad rather than a recycled version of the one he saw last week. It touches on what's called *multiple sources and multiple arguments*. Simply put, the more different sources that expose a subject to the same message, the more convinced the subject will become.

If, for example, you hear one women tell you how healthy it is to eat chocolate every day, you'll either believe or not, depending how the idea strikes you at the time. (And how long it's been since your last bar of—yum—Perugina!) However, if five different people approach you throughout the day and tell you a similar, but slightly different version of this argument, chances are it'll have serious impact on your belief system, and you are much more likely to adopt this delicious idea as your own.

Principle #15: Rhetorical Questions — *Interesting, Aren't They?*

The *rhetorical question* is really a statement disguised as a question. Pretty sneaky, isn't it? (Another example.) Not a new technique by any means, it was even mentioned in Aristotle's classic guide to oratorical skills, *The Art of Rhetoric* (circa 330 BC, first published in 1926). Television attorneys are known for using rhetorical questions during cross examination to pressure their opponents, throw them off balance, and add an air of veracity to their arguments. For example, "And isn't it true you stuck the dinner fork in his eye just minutes after you threw the cheese wheel at his head?" Other examples of this principle:

* Dial soap commercials asked, "Aren't you glad you use Dial? Don't you wish everyone did?"
* In 1926, newspaper ads for the laundry detergent Rinso asked, "Who else wants a whiter wash—with no hard work?"
* Rolaids posed the question, "How do you spell relief?"
* And W.B. Doner—the largest independently owned advertising agency in North America—is apparently a fan of the rhetorical, in its catchy, "What would you do for a Klondike Bar?" campaign. (Personally, I'd do plenty for anything covered in chocolate, but let's stay on topic here.)

This simple technique allows advertisers to make factual-sounding, possibly persuasive claims without having to support them with factual evidence or logical argument. Some research suggests that using rhetorical questions can *sometimes* change how people think, and modify their buying behavior. The idea is, if consumers aren't thinking carefully about an advertiser's message, slipping in a rhetorical question grabs their attention and encourages them to fire up some brain cells and think about the message.

According to McCroskey (1986), "The reason for this is due to our social training. When somebody asks us a question, it is required that we respond to it. To respond correctly requires that we understand the question."

Bottom line: The listener or reader makes a conscious attempt to consider the advertiser's message, which increases the likelihood of successful persuasion.

Respected communication researcher Dolf Zillmann conducted the first of only a few published studies on the topic in 1972. Several other researchers followed. And although the whole idea sounds great, there is, unfortunately, not much agreement as to the effectiveness of the technique.

Some say, "Yes! It works!" (Burkrant and Howard, 1984; Enzle and Harvey, 1982; Howard, 1990; Howard and Kerin, 1994; Petty, Cacioppo, and Heesaker, 1981; Swasy and Munch, 1985; Zillmann, 1972; Zillmann and Cantor, 1974). Results from other studies say, "Nope, it's not particularly effective in all situations." (Cantor, 1979; Munch, Boller, and Swasy, 1993; Munch and Swasy, 1988; Pentony, 1990.) In 1998, researchers Gayle,

Preiss, and Allen analyzed the currently available research on the topic and concluded that rhetorical questions have "no appreciable influence on persuasion." Other research suggests that the technique could make your audience feel pressured and persuaded, and therefore cause them to look more critically at your message and regard you as less of an authority on the topic (Swasy and Munch, 1985).

Sigh. With all this research, isn't there *anything* on which we can all agree regarding rhetorical questions? Perhaps just this: the use of rhetorical questions may be beneficial for *increasing message retention*. Questions designed to emphasize a point, rather than to persuade, are likely to cause your audience to remember your message. Makes sense, right? The more you think about something, the more brain cells you devote to it, and the more likely you are to remember it.

Principle #16: Evidence—
Quick! Sell Me the Facts!

Whenever I sit down to write an ad, I know that, unless I can convince you to believe me, you're not going to log into PayPal and make my bank account grow fatter. That means that my words are responsible for taking you from your present state of belief, disbelief, or ignorance, and convincing you that what I'm selling is worth more than the money in your pocket.

Did you ever think of it that way? It's a good context in which to hold your products and services. People buy from you when they *believe* what you are selling is of greater value than the dollars they need to exchange for it. For example, in my advertising workshop, I say, "Let's do a little experiment in consumer psychology." I hold up a #10 envelope with a big question mark printed on it, and ask, "Does anyone have a $20 bill?" Several people raise their hands. I choose one person, walk over to her, and ask the following question: "If I asked you to trade me your $20 for what's inside this envelope, what is the one question you might want to ask me before making the trade, knowing that once we make the deal, you can't get your money back?"

Invariably, the participant responds, "What's in the envelope?" No matter where in the country I deliver the workshop, when I make that offer, participants will always ask that same logical question: "What's in the envelope?"

What does this tell us? It tells us that consumers all think the same thing before making any purchase decision. They all want to know one thing before they exchange anything of value, whether it's time, materials, or money. They all want to know what *they're* going to get out of the deal. They all want to know the answer to the big question, "What's in it for me?" or the acronym, "WIIFM." Until they know the WIIFM, they're not only hesitant to make the deal, but they're also reluctant to even raise their hands in response to my question asking if they have a $20 bill! This hints at the *fear* that accompanies many buying decisions: the fear of loss. (Re-read that last sentence.)

Next—and notice the contrast with this experiment—I hold up a plastic bag with a $20 bill clearly visible. I asked the audience, "Who would like to trade their $1 bill for this bag containing a $20 bill?" Not surprisingly, dozens of hands spring up, as if I just offered to toss gold Krugerrands to the first person who can catch them. In this example, the audience—these *consumers*—demonstrated that once they *knew* the WIIFM, the benefit to them, they were much more likely to exchange their money for what was in the bag. This is the best way I know to demonstrate the foundational principle of advertising: telling your prospects the benefits of what you're selling. They must, must, must be convinced that what's in "your bag" is worth more than the money you ask for it, or the deal won't happen.

All right, so we know we have to convince our prospects of the value of what we're selling. To convince means to cause belief. So *how* do we get them to believe? One great, proven way is by offering persuasive evidence. Here's the definition of *evidence* in 19 words: "Any factual statement, object, or opinion not created by a source that is used by that source as support" (Reinhard, 1988). More simply, evidence can be facts, figures, testimonials, endorsements, research, charts, videos—you name it—as long as you, the advertiser, didn't create it yourself.

There's no doubt about it: Research concludes that evidence works, and works well. Advertisers who use solid evidence persuade more effectively than those who use poor evidence or none at all. Let's face it: You can't create an ad loaded with a slew of benefits and simply expect people to believe what you write. When they first see your ad, they know full well that you're trying to sell them. If what you're offering is something in which they're interested, they *want* to believe your claims. That's because believing your claims and purchasing your product may lead them to enjoy the benefits you're promising. It's like going to a personal development seminar and watching a professional speaker. You're not sitting there hoping the speaker screws up. You *want* him or her to perform well. You *want* him or her to speak powerfully, to *move* you, and perhaps even change your life for the better.

Likewise, if what you're selling promises to either to resolve a problem I'm experiencing or in some way better my life, I *want* to be convinced that it will work as you say it will. But at the same time—and this is why the cash register doesn't ring *every* time—*I don't want to be ripped off.* It's up to *you* to appeal effectively to my emotions to get me excited enough to spend the money. It's also up to you, especially for a costlier product, to supply enough reasoning so I can justify the expenditure of my money, thereby satisfying my adult sense of responsibility. Strong evidence can do this. In addition to its persuasive effects, evidence also creates a positive impression of your company as one that offers "legitimate" goods and services. (After all, they were backed by evidence!)

Evidence is most effective when we're faced with buying important or expensive goods or services. In these situations, we're primed to think carefully about our purchases and consider the arguments and issues involved. As a nice added benefit, deep, reasoned (central route) thinking can produce a long-term change in your prospect's attitude that's resistant to the sales messages of your competitors. Isn't that a nice benefit?

Interestingly enough, even peripheral (superficial) thinkers are influenced by strong evidence. When faced with facts and figures, testimonials and charts, these thinkers say, "Wow...look at all these facts and figures. It's got to be true!"

CA$HVERTISING Tip: In order to influence our peripheral-thinking friends, make sure you present your evidence in a clear and easy-to-grasp manner. Peripheral thinkers will not take the time to figure out what you're trying to say. They'll look at your data, and—boom!—make a decision as to what it means. Therefore, you should feature colorful charts and graphs, and facts, figures, and quotes from respected intellectuals and professionals.

Once a salesperson has you "cornered," he can unleash his full arsenal of sales techniques on you. In print ads, you have a limited amount of space to make your point, and a limited amount of time to grab your readers' attention and hold it throughout your sales pitch. The final principle exploits these time limitations by encouraging the reader to use psychologically powerful mental shortcuts called *heuristics.*

Principle #17: Heuristics—
Serving Billions of Lazy Brains Daily

First, let's overcome our fear of the strange word *heuristics*. Pronounced "hyu-RIS-tiks," it's a derivative of the Greek word *heuriskein* meaning "to discover." Heuristics pertain to the process of gaining (or discovering) knowledge, not by critical thinking and reasoning, but by intelligent guesswork. We referred to this process earlier by the less tongue-twisting term, *cues*, when we specifically discussed the six-cue CLARCCS model popularized by social psychologist Robert Cialdini.

Well, not to be outdone, researchers Stec and Bernstein (1999) put forth their own brand of persuasion heuristics, three of them to be exact: the *Length-Implies-Strength Heuristic*, the *Liking-Agreement Heuristic*—affectionately known as *Balance Theory*—and the *Consensus-Implies-Correctness Heuristic*. We'll explore only the first principle—*Length-Implies-Strength*—because we already covered the other two in our discussion of Cialdini's six weapons of influence: liking and comparison, respectively.

Let's face it: We humans are lazy creatures. Most of us prefer to take the quickest route to arriving at decisions, because doing so eliminates the hard work—the "pain" of thinking, and the need to consider all the complex or overwhelming details. If we can make a decision quickly, then we can get back to doing more fun stuff, such as watching ridiculous videos on YouTube. And when it comes to using our brains, for many of us, most *anything* is more pleasurable than engaging in deep thought. Inventor-genius Thomas Edison said it best: "There is no expedient to which a man will not go to avoid the labor of thinking."

Heuristic decision-making to the rescue! You see, if we're exposed to the right type of information, our "mental trains" will stay on their peripheral processing tracks and pull into the station fully prepared to make a decision in seconds or minutes instead of hours, days, or longer. In addition to Cialdini's six cues, there are a number of heuristics that psychologists and researchers have identified, but not all are as readily applicable in advertising. The following heuristic, however, is one of the most popular—and effective—and you can start using it immediately.

The Length-Implies-Strength Heuristic is a principle that exerts an influence similar to *evidence*. It's based on the assumption that a product or service is more likely to be viewed favorably if the ad is long and contains numerous, credible facts and figures. It causes your prospect to say, in effect, "Wow...look how much is here. It must be true." It's similar to listening to someone speak at length about a particular topic. Eventually, when you've heard enough—as long as the presentation was reasonably polished—you'd probably feel that the speaker knew what he was talking about. After all, "He went on for so long!" Of course length itself doesn't mean something is truthful, but that is exactly how this principle works.

Loading your ads with testimonials is one way to tune your prospects' brains to "Heuristic Channel #1." Another way is to write long, engaging copy. Not only does long copy give you more opportunities to persuade, but it also has the effect of causing prospects to believe that because there's so much copy, there must be something to it! This is the very essence of the Length-Implies-Strength heuristic.

How many photos of satisfied customers do you have? Put them in your ads, brochures, and sales letters, and on your Website. Show just *one* photo, and it communicates little more than you have *one* satisfied customer. Show dozens of them, and it produces a powerfully positive perception of credibility and certainty about your claims by quantity alone.

Remember my client Jay Siff of Moving Targets? He sends his prospects a four-page full-color brochure called "101 Success Stories." It contains—you guessed it—101 testimonials and photographs from clients who rave about his service. It impossible to not be impressed by this brochure. Even if you didn't read the rest of the information that accompanies this sales piece, you'd be instantly inclined to believe that the service he promotes actually works. Not only does it work like gangbusters—and yes, it really does—but even 101 people said so!

To promote my advertising workshop, I created a one-page, 8 1/2 × 14-inch flyer that I call my "Speak Out!" sheet. The page is divided into three narrow columns and is jam-packed with quotes from participants, including their names, business names, cities, and states. At the top of the page, in the upper left-hand corner, is my photograph. The big and bold headline, to its right, says:

Participants Speak Out!

Here's What they're Saying About

Drew Eric Whitman's CA$HVERTISING Workshop:

It's packed with so many glowing testimonials that by the time you're finished reading, or merely scanning this flyer, your head is spinning! You "know"—heuristically, at least—that there *must* be something to it.

How many good reasons can you give prospects to buy your product or service? Simple lists are powerful. In my work for Day-Timers, I gave prospects 22 good reasons why they should buy the great Day-Timer organizer. It hit them from most every angle. If you had even the slightest penchant for organizing your life, this list would (1) get you excited about the many benefits you'd enjoy, and (2) help convince you that the product has real merit because of the 22 reasons I listed to buy it.

Your prospect might be able to discount a few of the things you throw at them. But if you provide enough information, the Length-Implies-Strength heuristic will kick in and save the day. "Look how long this list is! Maybe a couple of these things aren't completely factual, but this one looks right...and this one is cool...and hey, this benefit would be helpful."

A politician stands in front of a crowd and pulls out a 50-page document that he proclaims contains more than 200 examples of how his opponent, Ted Torpy, flip-flopped on critical issues facing the nation. He cracks open the document and starts reading off one damning flip-flopped quote after another, vocally numbering each one in an effort to impress upon his audience the scope and problematic *quantity* of his opponent's worrisome trait. Not only will *what* he reads trouble his audience, but so will the sheer *number* of things read. (Never mind that 95 percent of the quotes were taken out of context, and some others factually fractured.)

But Mr. Politico doesn't stop there. No way. He next labels his opponent's collection of slippery statements, "Torpy's Tricky 200," and starts mentioning it in his print ads and TV commercials. He prints and binds the document and passes it out at rallies. He converts it to a PDF and offers it for instant download on his Website. People read the first few pages, quickly thumb through the rest, and *clearly* see that each "flip-flop" quote is boldly numbered. Not 1 in 1,000 readers do any fact checking. Who has time for that? So "Torpy's Tricky 200" starts to get the play this politician knew it would, and it eventually takes on a life of its own. T-shirts. YouTube videos. Bumper stickers. Blogs. Few people read the entire document, but who needs to? You can see there are 200 quotes in it! It must be saying something!

Poor Ted Torpy. The latest victim of heuristic homicide. He was "cued" to death. In retrospect, he never really understood exactly how the strategy worked against him. And speaking of the word *heuristics*, interestingly enough, not 1 in 100 of those who voted against him had ever even *heard* the word before.

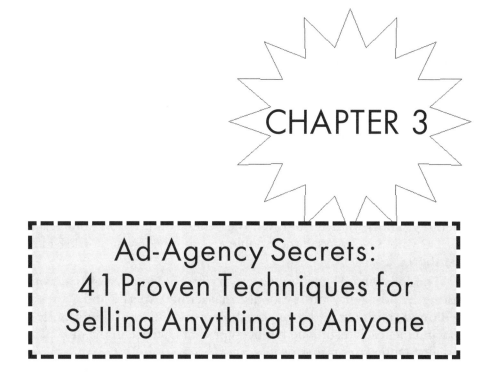

CHAPTER 3

Ad-Agency Secrets:
41 Proven Techniques for
Selling Anything to Anyone

Don't reinvent the light bulb...just switch it on!

Thomas Edison held an unbelievable 1,093 patents. Not for ridiculous, useless trinkets similar to 99 percent of the contestants on ABC's reality show *American Inventor*, but for revolutionary, life-changing discoveries that influence the lives of billions of people worldwide: the phonograph, incandescent light, motion picture camera, automatic telegraph system, universal stock ticker, electric vote recorder, mimeograph, telephone receiver, and so many others.

And talk about persistence! While working to improve the incandescent electrical lamp (existing ones didn't burn long enough or were too bright for small spaces), Edison and his associates tested more than 3,000 different theories and thousands of plant materials.

"Before I got through," Edison said, "I tested no fewer than 6,000 vegetable growths, and ransacked the world for the most suitable filament material." *Whew!* At what point would *you* have given up?

"Fascinating, Drew, but why the history lesson?" To make a point. If for some wacky reason you wanted to build your own light bulb, instead of spending years duplicating Edison's thousands of failed experiments, wouldn't it be wiser to read his lab notes and see how *he* did it? How he discovered that a carbonized bamboo filament burns slowly enough in a vacuum to produce more than 1,200 hours of reliable light?

Of course! You'd simply duplicate what he did, rapidly produce a long-lasting light bulb, and get on with your life. Whenever you study someone who was successful at a task you're preparing to attempt, you pave yourself an incredible shortcut to success.

The same applies to your advertising. There's no need for *you* to spend years and thousands of your own dollars experimenting, when thousands of Edisons have already done it for you. If you like experimenting, knock yourself out. On the other hand, if you want results *now*, why not save yourself the trouble and simply do what works? Life's too short.

The following 41 techniques are backed by decades of real-world testing by ad-agency professionals, marketing experts, and scores of dedicated consumer and social psychologists. And most importantly to you and me, each technique has been proven effective in the only place it really matters: *the real world*.

Fact: By the time you've finished reading *CA$HVERTISING*, you'll know more about how to create powerfully effective, money-making advertising than 99 percent of your competitors will know in their entire careers—*guaranteed*. Now let's get started.

Ad-Agency Secret #1:
The Psychology of Simplicity

Stop reading this book. Because if you don't follow the advice of this first lesson, no matter how wonderful your product, your advertising will likely fail. Miserably. It's the foundation for everything else I'm going to teach you. It's like telling a first-time boxing student that lesson #1 is "How to stand." Boring? Maybe, but if he skips this lesson because "It's boring!" he'll probably get his head blasted off his shoulders the first time he steps into the ring. And although the lesson might be obvious, it's still vitally important. If you treat this first topic lightly, your ads (and your business)—just like that newbie boxer—will likely suffer one painful knock-out after another. It's as simple as that.

Fact: The goal of advertising is to get people to act. And the tools we use to create printed advertising (as opposed to TV and radio) are *words* (as opposed to sound and moving images). So, doesn't it logically follow that, in order for our ads to be effective, we need to use our *words* effectively? Of course. And using words effectively means we must write so our audience *understands* what we're saying. As simple as it is, my friend, you've just learned the #1 key to all effective written communication: *Write so people can understand*. This idea is based on Consumer Psychology Principle #11, "Message Organization."

> Write to the chimpanzee brain. Simply. Directly.
>
> —Eugene Schwartz

Let's face it: You could have the greatest invention since indoor plumbing, but if no one understands what the heck you're trying to say about it, you may as well have the crappiest one. What's the difference? In either case, they're *not* buying. Effective communication doesn't happen until the people to whom you're trying to communicate *understand* your message. Just because you're running an ad in a newspaper or magazine, or your Website is online, doesn't mean you're communicating *effectively*. You *are* advertising, I'll give you that. But until someone reads and *understands* it, you're just talking to yourself. And you don't need to spend a penny to do that. (I talk to myself quite often, so I know.)

It's one thing to *try* to write simply; quite another to actually *do* it. And short of doing your own testing—asking friends, neighbors, and family members to read your sales copy—it's tough to get a real sense of just how readable your copy *really* is. Dr. Rudolf Flesch to the rescue!

The Flesch Reading Ease Formula

In his book, *The Art of Plain Talk*, Dr. Rudolph Flesch analyzes what makes writing easy or difficult to read. In the early 1940s he developed a formula to determine readability that we still use today, nearly 70 years later. If you use Microsoft Word, accessing your Flesch Reading Ease Score (FRES) is just a button-click away. Based on a scale of 1 to 100, the higher your score, the easier the reading. If you're a math lover, or you just want to understand how the formula works, here are the five steps. (If you're a masochist, you can calculate the formula manually.)

Step #1—Count the words: Count as single words contractions, hyphenated words, abbreviations, figures, symbols and their combinations. For example, *shouldn't, extra-rich, TV, 12, &, $17, 5%*.

Step #2—Count the syllables: Count the syllables in words as you'd pronounce them. Count abbreviations, figures, symbols, and their combinations as one-syllable words. If a word has two accepted pronunciations, use the one with fewer syllables. Unsure? Grab a dictionary.

Step #3—Count the sentences: Count as a sentence each full unit of speech that's separated by a period, colon, semicolon, question mark, exclamation point, or dash. Ignore paragraph breaks, colons, semicolons, initial capitals, or dashes occurring *within* a sentence.

Step #4—Determine the average number of syllables per word: Divide the total syllables by the number of words.

Step #5—Figure the average number of words per sentence: Divide the number of words by the number of sentences.

The result—*whew!*—is your readability score.

> Your ad gets only a fraction of their intelligence...people won't study your ad carefully. They can't be bothered. And so you have to make your ads simple.
>
> —John Caples

Flesch gives an excellent example of how complexity affects score. The sentence, "John loves Mary" scores 92—*very easy*. Now let's crank up the difficulty. "John has a profound affection for Mary." Not quite as simply said or as specific, is it? Score: 67. Not *too* bad, but definitely headed in the wrong direction. Now the worst: "Even though John is not normally given to a display of his deeper emotions, he allegedly has developed a profound affection for Mary, as compared to the more equable feelings he seems to have for Lucy, Fran, and, to a lesser extent, Sue." Ugh...what a wordy mess! Score: 32—*difficult*. See what happened? It degraded into vagary, complexity, and added a whopping 36 hard-to-read words. It's now comparable in reading difficulty to the *Harvard Law Review*. You can be sure that Romeo never expressed his affection for Juliet this way!

How do the scores translate into school grades? According to Flesch, here are the rankings:

If Your Score Is:	Then Your Grade Is:
0–30	College grad
30–50	College
50–60	10th to 12th
60–70	8th and 9th
70–80	7th grade
80–90	6th grade
90–100	5th grade

If your score's *too* low, Flesch suggests to "shorten the words and sentences until you get the score you want." In fact, for best readability, he recommends sentence length of approximately 11 words. You should also refer to people (Bob, Eileen, he, him, she, her, and so on) at least 14 times in every 100 words.

Not to be outdone by Dr. Flesch, other researchers started popping up like springtime crocuses with their own readability indices. There's the Fog Index, which tells you the number of years of education your readers need in order to understand you; the Flesch-Kincaid Index, used by the U.S. Department of Defense to check readability of its mind-numbingly dry forms and publications; the McLaughlin "SMOG" Formula, developed in 1969 by Harry McLaughlin, former editor of the London newspaper the *Mirror*; the Forcast formula, developed for assessing U.S. Army technical manuals and forms; and others.

Phooey! There's no need for you to calculate all this yourself. I let my computer do the work—the very same computer I'm using right now to type the words you're reading.

CA$HVERTISING Tip: Did you notice what just happened? By commenting on the *context* of what's going on, specifically, you reading this book, teamed with the implication that I'm "on the other side of the writing" using my computer, I've shaken you out of your reading routine a bit, haven't I? Chances are you felt somewhat more "present" to what's going on because I called your attention to it. I've shifted the focus from the topic being discussed to commenting on present events outside of the topic. Now, stop reading this side note (I just did it again!) and jump back to the topic.

Here are two test paragraphs that talk about the same offer. Read both and see which you enjoy reading most. Which is easiest? Which is most clear? After you read both, I'll tell you what the computer analysis said.

Test Paragraph #1

"Would you like to make $10,000 a month making your own ice cream? (My wife Lindsay and I do. In fact, sometimes we make thousands more. We showed our friend Steve, and now he makes an additional $4,300 every month with ease.) Then keep reading. Because by the time you're finished this letter, *you'll* know how. In fact, I'm going to spill the beans and tell you over 48 insider secrets that not one person in 1,000 knows. Any *one* of these secrets is worth the cost of this entire package."

Test Paragraph #2

"If you wish to acquire vast financial resources, please pay close attention to the following information. Numerous individuals in the frozen confectionary industry have, for years, kept closely guarded secrets that reveal the fast route to establishing yourself as a much-in-demand artisan ice cream producer in a ridiculously short period of time. While they shudder to think about passing on such data to the general public, I am more than willing to proffer said privileged information to you."

Okay, now let's take a quick look at the stats.

Paragraph #	Sentences Per Paragraph	Words Per Sentence	Characters Per Word	Flesch Reading Ease Score (1-100: Higher = Better)	Flesch-Kincaid Grade Level
1	7.0	13.1	4.1	72.1	6.4
2	3.0	25.3	5.3	34.1	14.7

Wow, what a difference! Although Test Paragraph #1 contains more sentences, Test Paragraph #2 features much longer sentences...over 12 words longer each. Longer sentences mean longer thoughts, which require more mental effort to follow them. The more you ask people to think, the more likely you'll lose them.

What's more, Test Paragraph #1 uses shorter words. But where's the biggest difference? In the Flesch Reading Ease Score and Flesch-Kincaid Grade Level. With its score of 72.1 (remember, 100 is best), Test Paragraph #1 ranks with the easy-to-understand speaking you'd hear watching your favorite movie. A 6th grader should be able to read and understand this passage. By contrast, Test Paragraph #2 scores similarly to the *New York Review of Books,* and is far more difficult for the average person to read and comprehend. With its low score of 34.1, it's considered "college" reading level. And according to the U.S. Department of Education, National Center for Education Statistics: (1) In 2007 only about 30 percent of 25- to 29-year-olds had completed a bachelor's degree or higher, and (2) Approximately 3.4 million 16- to 24-year-olds were high school dropouts.

Regardless of your prospects' educational background, short words and short sentences make reading easier for everybody. (Of course, don't use *all* three-letter words and super-short sentences and paragraphs. Vary them so your copy sounds natural, not robotic. A good rule of thumb is that about 70 to 80 percent of your copy should consist of one-syllable words.)

The software also checks for what Flesch calls *definite words.* These are nouns, proper names, pronouns, verbs, and specifics. The more specific you are, the less figuring your reader has to do in order to understand your message. "Joey ate chocolate" is more definite than saying, "Someone did something."

DON'T SAY:

"Become financially successful."

DO SAY:

"You'll make up to $2,495 every week."

DON'T SAY:

"Want your entire body to look more appealing?"

DO SAY:

"**MEN!** Do you want a rippling, rock-hard stomach?

WOMEN! Do you want lean, luscious thighs?"

Whoopee! Those headlines would knock 'em dead! So follow these four simple prescriptions for highly readable writing.

Prescription #1: Use Short, Simple Words

"As I proceed to issue the following informational text, I hope that you understand that the vast majority of individuals will, without question, proceed to issue forth a counter-opinion predicated upon the fact that their life experiences dictate just the opposite guidelines as those issued to them in good gesture. Unfortunately, in an atmosphere in which educational disciplines are of utmost importance, I hasten to dictate the potential loss of data acquisition; however this is indeed the perceived and forecasted outcome of this quite burdensome situation."

Did you enjoy reading that last paragraph? Probably not. Why? Because it sounds as if it were written by a constipated Harvard Law professor. And, according to the *McLaughlin "SMOG" Formula*, it's written on a post-graduate degree reading level, which is comparable to IRS code. Yawn. Unfortunately, more people write this way than you'd believe. This is especially unfortunate when the person writes *advertising*! But there's a good reason why people write that way: *that's how many people were taught to write!*

In school, we were taught to write as adults. To talk with "big" words. So the word *tired* became *enervated*. *Hungry* became *famished*. *Big* became *elephantine*. *Stubborn* became *recalcitrant*. *Evil* became *nefarious*. Sigh...you get the idea.

But do you see what has happened to you and me? Because we were trained to write this way, we tend to write this way whenever we write *anything*. This means that every time we write an ad, brochure, sales letter, e-mail, or Web page, we are, in effect, flushing our money down the toilet. Why? *Because nobody understands what the $@#!* we're talking about!*

Forget those annoying $10 words and phrases you were taught in school and business. You know the ones I mean: *and you'll enjoy same, the aforementioned benefits, you can liken this to, herein are 10 reasons*, and any other of those tired, stodgy expressions. Just be clear, natural, and simple.

Prescription #2:
The Shorter Your Sentences, the Better

It's easier to read short sentences, isn't it? Sure is! It's quick! Lively! Exciting, too, wouldn't you say? Chop your sentences down with a big ol' ax. You'll rivet people's eyes to your sales copy, encouraging them to read more.

Rule of thumb: Express only *one* thought in a sentence, no more. Use your *next* sentence to say the next thing. Why? Because it's much easier for your readers to process and understand just one thought at a time. And because everything you say is important, you want them to understand each of your sales points, don't you? Of course.

So do as the good Dr. Flesch suggests: (1) Use shorter words—70 to 80 percent of them should consist of just one syllable, and (2) write shorter sentences—aim for about 11 words each. People will read more. The more they read, the greater your chance of persuading them to buy. The more they buy, the more money you make. Any questions?

Prescription #3: The Short, Short Paragraph Trick

Here's a great trick used by today's top copywriters to keep people reading and moving ahead at a quick pace. You simply ask a question or make a quick statement, and then answer the question or continue the thought in the next paragraph in just a few words. Here's an example.

Dear Bob,

Would you like to know a secret way of making money by simply watching TV?

I thought so.

Now let me explain...

Not only does this short-paragraph trick move your readers' eyes down the page, but it also quickens their pace and makes your ad or letter *look* much more inviting. (As opposed to a big, solid page full of text.) Don't overdo this technique, or your writing will look too mechanical. Limit your regular paragraphs to about four or five short sentences.

Drew Alan Kaplan knows this trick well. In his wildly popular direct-mail catalog of high-tech electronic gadgets, Kaplan writes extremely engaging copy that sells products like hotcakes. He took a tiny business run from his cramped dorm room at UCLA, and grew it into a slamming 400-person sales machine that moved, for example, 450,000 radar detectors, 250,000 stereo equalizers, 100,000 subwoofers, and 900,000 bread makers. (Yours truly bought a radar detector, and I'm still baking fresh bread today. Yep, I'm a sucker for great copy.) In virtually every one of his full-page catalog ads, he starts the first paragraph with sentences consisting of only two to four words. Of the eight products I just now reviewed on his Website, six of them use this technique:

* "I confess."
* "We're free."
* "It's tough."
* "This is important."
* "S.W.A.T. teams use them."
* "It's a problem."

It's a fast and easy way to lure people into your copy, and it's supported by some of the biggest names in advertising.

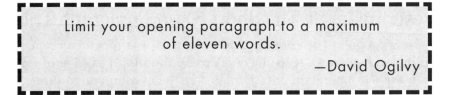

Limit your opening paragraph to a maximum of eleven words.

—David Ogilvy

Prescription #4:
Pile on the Personal Pronoun Personality

Finally, I want you to load your copy with pronouns, such as *you, me, I, he, she, him, they,* and *them.* Be especially generous with the words *you* and *I.* Pronouns give your copy a warm, human flavor that people notice instantly. It helps turn your *mass* communication into *personal* communication, the most effective kind. In fact, It's nearly impossible to overuse the word *you* in well-written copy. Generously sprinkle it throughout like shaking parmesan cheese on a pizza. Start sentences with it! End sentences with it! Blow it up in big type! Put it in your headline! Ask questions and make statements using pronouns:

"Do *you*...Can *you*...Would *you*...Should *you*...May I ask *you* a question? May I ask *your* advice? Can I get *your* opinion? Did *you* know...Let me tell *you*...I think *you'll* like this idea..."

Okay, let's review what you learned so far.

YOU LEARNED that in order for your advertising to be successful, you must first be aware of what blocks your readers from understanding your message.

YOU LEARNED that your readers don't care about your big vocabulary, only what you can do for them. That means you use shorter words, sentences, and paragraphs.

YOU LEARNED that advertising copy doesn't have to follow all the rules of a college composition. Your copy has one job: to sell, Sell, SELL!

YOU LEARNED how to use questions to draw people into your copy and keep them reading. Right?

YOU LEARNED how to use pronouns, such as the words *you* and *I* to make your copy sound personal. And you now know an easy way to determine the readability of your copy by using the Flesch formula.

CA$HVERTISING Tip: Do you see how I kept repeating the words *you learned* in the five preceding paragraphs? Paragraph leaders are a powerful way to increase reading speed and establish an upbeat tempo in your ads. The repetition increases the reader's perception of volume, and, according the Length-Implies-Strength heuristic discussed in Chapter 2—can help boost credibility. Other effective paragraph leaders are, "We Guarantee...," "We Promise...," "You'll Receive...," and similar. And even if you really *didn't* learn all those things (despite my parroting "you learned"), the mere repetition of the word can cause you to doubt your own feelings because "it's so confident...it's so specific...and there are so many of them."

Ad-Agency Secret #2:
Bombard Your Readers With Benefits

Let's now talk about the million-dollar secret for getting inside your readers' heads: *benefits*. Play close attention. If you don't incorporate this idea in *all* of your advertising, you may as well pack up now and try a different business that sells to beings other than humans.

Remember our discussion about the Life-Force 8 from Chapter 1? As you may recall, the LF8 are the primary human desires that are hard-wired into our brains. These are powerful wants we're biologically driven to fulfill, no matter who we are, where we live, or what we do. If your product or service can satisfy one of these desires—or any of the nine secondary wants—you have the making of killer benefit claims that can start the sales ball rolling. The fact is, if you don't put benefits in your advertising, whether it's an ad, brochure, sales letter, Website, or *whatever*, then kiss your money goodbye!

Now, before you start puckering up, let's examine what a *benefit* is, in advertising terms. Benefits are those things that offer your prospects value. And as the word implies, they're things that directly benefit not *you*, but your *prospect*. Is a benefit the same as a feature? No! You *must* learn the distinction. A *feature* is simply a component of a product or service. For example:

PRODUCT: Rolls-Royce Phantom Coupé

FEATURE: Top-grade, hand-selected seat leathers.

BENEFIT: Luxurious comfort in all climates.

FEATURE: Deep-pile Wilton lamb's wool carpeting.

BENEFIT: The rich softness underfoot and lush elegance.

FEATURE: 453 horsepower, 6.75-liter V-12 engine.

BENEFIT: Power, control, supreme reliability.

FEATURE: Bold, dignified styling with artist Charles Sykes's "Spirit of Ecstasy" flying proudly on the hood.

BENEFIT: The feeling of power, success, and that you've "arrived."

Get it? The features are the *attributes*. The *benefits* are what you *get* from those attributes. The benefits are what entice people to buy. Remember, the entire time people are reading your ads, they're consciously thinking, "WIIFM?": "What's In It For Me?" In fact, they can't turn it off! Over and over and over and over. It's like a corrupt MP3 file that never stops repeating. By loading your ads with benefits, telling your prospects how and what they gain, how their lives will improve, you're answering the "WIIFM" they're continually trying to satisfy. And when you do, their desire for your product increases, and you're on your way to making a sale.

> Consumers buy based on what the product will do for them, not on what ingredients it has.
>
> —Newspaper Association of America

In my workshop, I drive the point home with a popular (and often hilarious) two-person interaction called the "Feature-Benefit Exercise." I pair up participants and ask one to play the role of the seller, and the other the prospect. The seller starts by telling the prospect one feature of his product or service. Then I instruct the prospect to respond with a loud and annoyed "BIG DEAL! What's in it for me?" And to convey just how worthless it is to state only the product's *features*, I instruct the prospect to simultaneously throw her hands in the air and give a look of pure disgust while shouting this. The seller must begin his reply with the words, "You benefit by...."

Here's a typical interaction.

Business Owner: "My product is an ink-jet printer. One feature is multiple ink tanks."

Prospect: "BIG DEAL! What's in it for me?!" (Arms flailing overhead.)

Business Owner: "You benefit by saving big money because you don't have to replace the entire cartridge when only one ink color runs out."

Prospect: "That's nice...I spend a fortune for ink with my current printer.

Business Owner: "Feature: 500-sheet tray."

Prospect: "BIG DEAL! What's in it for me?!" (Annoyed look of disgust.)

Business Owner: "You benefit by not having to fill the paper tray as often. Most other printers hold half as much."

Prospect: "Sounds like my printer; it's a pain to keep filling it."

Business Owner: "Feature: Ultra-draft mode button"

Prospect: "BIG DEAL! What's in it for me?!"

Business Owner: "You benefit by saving serious money on ink because the Ultra-Draft mode uses 50 percent less ink than other printers' ordinary draft mode."

The room usually erupts with laughter as dozens of prospects shout, with annoyed faces and frantic gestures of impatience and dissatisfaction. By the end of the exercise, the sellers know exactly how to sell their product. After all, they've been beaten down by prospects who've been given the okay to express what prospects are always thinking anyway!

Sorry, but people are *not* interested in your new equipment (only if it benefits *them*), or that you're celebrating your 10th anniversary (unless you're slashing your prices). Likewise, the photos of your staff might be all warm and fuzzy, but until you've poured on the benefits, they won't do a damned thing to make your cash register ring. Pictures of your newborn baby Tabatha? Forget it! Snapshot of your new cat Lu Lu Lemieux? Please! *Benefits* are what your prospects really care about. Benefits tap into Consumer Psychology Principle #5: The Means-End Chain we covered in Chapter 2, which suggests to always focus on the core benefits and positive end results. *Loading your advertising with benefits is the key to all successful advertising.*

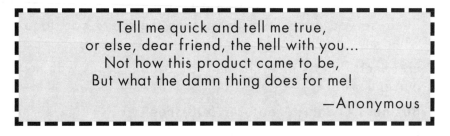

> Tell me quick and tell me true,
> or else, dear friend, the hell with you...
> Not how this product came to be,
> But what the damn thing does for me!
>
> —Anonymous

Ad-Agency Secret #3: Put Your Biggest Benefit in Your Headline

Talk about information overload! Estimates say we're exposed to anywhere from 247 ads per day (*Consumer Reports*) to more than 3,000 (Newspaper Association of America). If we're to stand any chance of convincing, persuading, motivating, selling, we must, must, *MUST* cut through the clutter! The easiest way to do this is to always—without exception—put your biggest benefit in your headline.

> Unless your headline sells your product, you have wasted 90 percent of your money.
>
> —David Ogilvy

Ad-Agency Secrets

Did you know that 60 percent of all people who read ads typically read headlines and no more? They skim until they "stub their eyeballs" on something that interests them. That means that about 60 percent of those that see your ad read only the first few words. Yikes!

Solution: Put the one thing that's most important to them in the place where they're most likely to see it: your headline. For example, let's say you're writing a headline for your restaurant workshop that teaches waiters and waitresses how to boost their income.

DON'T SAY:

"Attention Food Servers: New Workshop Teaches You the Tricks of the Trade!"

DO SAY:

"Attention Food Servers: New Workshop Teaches You How to Boost Your Tips by 512%...or Your Money Back!"

If you're an award-winning interior designer specializing in making ordinary houses look like beautiful model homes:

DON'T SAY:

"Louise Taylor Designs Homes of Distinction"

Distinction? This claim is too amorphous; it creates no mental movies, and gives your prospects nothing to grasp. Instead:

DO SAY:

"Award-Winning Interior Designer Louise Taylor Turns Your House Into a Gorgeous Model Home for Less than You Ever Dreamed Possible!"

Ahhh...now we have a *real* idea of what Louise will do. She's telling us the #1 reason why someone would hire her: to make their house look beautiful.

Is your camera shop drowning in rolls of film because everyone's going digital?

DON'T SAY:

"Capturing the Best Times of Your Life Is Now a Snap!"

DO SAY:

"GIANT FILM SALE!

93

All Rolls of 35mm Color Film are 25% Off—This Week Only!"

Are you a bakery looking to hook customers with your heavenly new "to-die-for" fudge-filled pastry?

DON'T SAY:

"Come In and Sample Our Latest Confectionary Masterpiece!"

DO SAY:

"Attention Chocolate Lovers: Now Sink Your Teeth Into the 8 1/2-Pound Fudge-Devil Volcano Pie—Absolutely Free!"

See the simplicity? Your headline should immediately select the audience you want to hook. By contrast, I saw an ad in a local shopper paper for a lighting supply store that featured the headline, "We'll Help You Brighten Up Your Life and Save Big!" Ugh, what a waste. Why? Because it does nothing to select its audience. The ad could be for paint, window cleaning, or even antidepressants! Instead, how about the ridiculously simple headline, "Need Lamps?" Think about it. Who would be attracted to a headline that says "Need Lamps?" Someone who needs lamps, of course! The audience, in this case, is perfectly selected. There's no guessing for whom it's meant.

> The headline is the "ticket on the meat." Use it to flag down readers who are prospects for the kind of product you are advertising.
>
> —David Ogilvy

Question: Is a longer or shorter headline more effective? Let's again turn to psychology. Researchers have conducted hundreds of tests to see just how much the average person can effectively "take in," or pay attention to. The results from all studies are similar. The average Joe or Jane can process a maximum of five to nine numbers (George A. Miller, *The Magical Number Seven, Plus or Minus Two*, 1956) in a "single act of attention." Ever wonder why phone numbers are seven digits? Bell Telephone wanted to make them long enough to accommodate the most variations, but short enough that people would remember them.

Word-wise, most people can grasp the meaning of five to six words in a single glance.

So does this mean that short headlines get higher readership? Yes. And studies confirm it. That's because the number of words in a headline affects reading speed, and therefore affects how much of the headline is read.

Here's an example to drive this point home. If you saw the newspaper headline "WAR!" it takes no effort whatsoever to read and process it, does it? As long as you recognize the word, it communicates its meaning instantly. That's why the readership is so high. Your eyeballs simply have to hit the word, and it's as good as read. As you add words, you're moving in the opposite direction of speed, work, ease, and understanding.

Take, for example, the headline, "War Was Declared Yesterday by the Blordoni Tribe in the Nation of Kimbootu Against Its Historically More Aggressive Southern Neighbors, the WoopWoops." It simply takes more time and effort to pore through a longer headline such as this, despite the silly tribal names. It forces you to *think* more (and we know most people would rather have cavities drilled than do that), and it adds more opportunities to get lost in meaning and boredom. That's why short headlines get higher readership.

> Short headlines enjoy higher readership than long headlines. As headlines grow, readership shrinks.
>
> —Starch Research

But before you grab an ax and start chopping down your headlines like an oak tree, realize that well-written *long* headlines can be—and often are—remarkably effective. In fact, some long-copy direct-response ads use extremely long headlines that often flow into extremely long subheads, creating a head/sub introduction dozens of words long!

A classic study of 2,500 ads appearing in the *Saturday Evening Post* was conducted from 1939 to 1940 by researcher Harold J. Rudolph. The results show that the shorter the headline, the greater the readership.

How Many Words in the Headline?	How Many People Read the Entire Headline?
Up to 3	87.3%
4–6	86.3%
7–9	84%
10–12	82.5%
13+	77.9%

In this study, the average readership of the shortest headline is about 1/7th better than the longest. We see the biggest drop in headlines with more than 12 words. According to Rudolf, "These findings, obviously, cannot be interpreted as an indication that a headline, to be consistently well read, need to only be short. Headline *content* is undoubtedly the major element affecting readership."

The flip side? A short headline isn't necessarily an *effective* headline. You can struggle just as much writing three words as you would 15, and your ad could *still* flop. Oh, sure, you'd likely get higher readership with the three-word headline because it takes no effort to read it, but that doesn't mean you chose the *right* words. According to David Ogilvy, longer headlines sell more products.

"Okay, Drew. Now I'm even more confused!" Alright...let's simplify:

1. *Always* put your biggest benefit in your headline.
2. If you can write two equally effective headlines, the shorter one will likely be read by more people, all other variables being the same.

For the purposes of practicality, *never* ignore rule #1, and keep rule #2 in mind to maximize readership when creating your next ad. There, don't you feel better?

Ad-Agency Secret #4:
Crank up the Scarcity

Your ad is your salesperson. And in my seminar, I give an example of a salesperson whom no business should ever tolerate. In a dry, boring, and monotone voice, I say, "Now you just take your time making the purchase decision. No need to decide right away. Certainly this product will be available in the future whenever you'd like to buy it."

Do you see a problem here? By suggesting there's no need to act now, that salesperson gives your prospects no incentive to buy *now*. We're talking about *human inertia*. Simply put, inertia is an object's resistance to a change in its current state of motion. Like sitting on a couch watching *Seinfeld* reruns—talk about inertia! It sometimes takes a miracle to get up, change your clothes, and go run on the treadmill.

As advertisers, we need to motivate people to take action *right now*. We don't want them to wait, or think about it, or put off the decision until the "later" that never comes.You want them to whip out their credit cards and order *now*. And it's not simply a matter of *asking* for the order—any good salesperson knows to do that. It's a matter of getting your prospect to take action *when the offer is presented to them*. And you do it by creating the perception of scarcity with powerful deadlines.

Tell people they can't have something and they want it more than ever. Remember our discussion of CLARCCS, the "Six Weapons of Influence?" The final "S" in that acronym—as you may recall—stands for *scarcity*, a powerful motivator. And it's the fear of loss that gives deadlines their power.

Can you imagine creating a powerful ad, filled with excellent copy, wonderful graphics, the perfect appeal; your pricing is dead-on, it's loaded with amazing testimonials, and it's running in a publication that you know will bring excellent response. The only thing you missed is including a deadline. And it doesn't matter whether you use a "hard" deadline (featuring a specific cut-off date), such as "Sale Ends August 21st," or a "soft" deadline, such as "Quantities are Strictly Limited"; the *absence* of a deadline conveys that your offer is always available. And this, more than anything else, connotes that there's no need to buy now; that there's plenty to go around.

What do you think would happen if, starting tomorrow, all the world's salespeople began ending their presentations with the following phrase:

"You don't need to buy this now. Take your time deciding. I'll get back to you in the future to see what you've decided." It would spell economic collapse on a scale the world has never known.

Advertising is persuasion. And the most critical time to persuade is when you're asking for action. Always feature deadlines to discourage response-killing human inertia. There's no skill involved. It couldn't be easier. But boy, is it ever powerful. Simply include standard phrases such as the following:

* Call Before April 5th
* Supplies Are Strictly Limited
* Offer Expires May 15
* Price Guaranteed Only Until August 3
* Offer Good Only Before 4 p.m.
* Seating Is Limited to 50 Participants
* NO Rain Checks Will Be Issued
* Good Only for the First 50 Callers

...and whatever other variations you can dream up. If you haven't been using deadlines, start tapping psychologist Robert Cialdini's Weapon of Influence #6, scarcity, and you'll immediately see the difference it makes in your response.

Ad-Agency Secret #5: 22 Psychologically Potent Headline Starters

Reading headlines is a lot like driving and reading signs. If you see a sign pointing in the direction you're interested in traveling, you'll stay on the road and keep motoring ahead. Otherwise, you'll turn off and look for a road that takes you where you want to go. Likewise, a headline that interests you will keep you reading. If the copy's strong enough, perhaps you'll also dig into your pocket and fork over some cash. Otherwise, you'll quickly take another route: glance at the other ads, turn the page, or click to another Website. In which case, to the advertiser, you're gone forever.

That's why it's critical that your headline do two things: (1) grab their attention, and (2) motivate them to keep reading. If it doesn't do *both*, you could be giving away free gold bars, and most people wouldn't notice. That's why *word choice* is so important. Fortunately, with the advice in Ad Agency Secret #3 "Put Your Biggest Benefit in

Your Headline," you know *what* to put in your headline. Now let's talk about *how* to say it.

> There are four important qualities that a good headline may possess. They are: 1. Self-interest. 2. News. 3. Curiosity. 4. Quick, easy way.
>
> — John Caples

Who isn't interested in themselves? To appeal to a consumer's self-interest, simply write a headline that promises a personal benefit: whiter teeth, higher income, healthier body, better relationships, and any others, especially those that tap into the Life-Force 8 desires discussed in Chapter 1.

People read the newspaper for news and other information. We're naturally interested in what's new, what's going on around us. Any time you can express your benefit with a news flavor, you add an extra zing that's very appealing. Your "news" can be as simple as announcing the release or availability of your product, and the way it benefits your buyer. Or, for an extra touch of timeliness, tie your ad into current events, weather, sports, or anything topical. "ATTENTION LOS ANGELES: Present This Coupon Below and Burgerilla Will Donate 10 Percent of Your Burger Purchases to Help Earthquake Victims—Now Through Friday."

Curious? Most people are. And a well-constructed headline can stir up enough curiosity to motivate them to keep reading, as in most of the following headlines. However, please don't get cutesy or clever with headlines that don't target the right audience, simply to hook eyeballs. The best example of this is the headline "SEX!" for ads that have as much to do with sex as do ads for PVC patio furniture. You don't simply want *lots* of eyeballs; you want the *right* eyeballs.

The following 22 tested headline starters can be used for most any product or service. Simply replace the example wording with words relevant to your business.

1. FREE: "Free Book Shows You How to Write Sneaky Advertising That Practically Forces People to Send You Money!"
2. NEW: "Powerful New Seminar Teaches Flea Marketers the Power of 'Flea-Psych' to Drive People Into a Buying Frenzy"

3. AT LAST: "At Last...A Bakery That Uses Only Organic Sugar, Flour, Milk, and Eggs!"

4. THIS: "This New Invention Stops Any Attacker in His Tracks Without a Gun, Knife, or Black Belt in Karate."

5. ANNOUNCING: "Announcing the Hottest New Sandwich Craze From Southern California: The Malibu Crust Pocket!"

6. WARNING! "WARNING! Some Dog Groomers Wrap a Noose Around Your Dog's Neck!"

7. JUST RELEASED: "Just Released: Psychologist's Study Reveals Little-Known Speaking Patterns That Immediately Put Rude Salespeople in Their Place."

8. NOW: "Now You Can Stop Any Attacker Without Guns, Knives, or a Black Belt in Karate."

9. HERE'S: "Here's How a 95-Pound Granny Made a 275-Pound Psychopathic Killer Cry Like a Baby for its Rattle...."

10. THESE: "These Three Very Italian Men Make a Pizza to Kill For."

11. WHICH OF: "Which of These Hot Bodies Would YOU Like to Show Off?"

12. FINALLY: "Finally...a Self-Improvement Seminar That Moves, Empowers, and Transforms You for Life!"

13. LOOK: "LOOK! Now You Can Buy Cotton Candy Machines at Wholesale Prices."

14. PRESENTING: "Presenting the Easiest Way Ever Developed to Learn the Piano."

15. INTRODUCING: "Introducing the Only Water Ice Stand in Philly that Uses Real Fresh Fruit."

16. HOW: "How to Sing Like an American Idol in 90 Days or Less—Guaranteed."

17. AMAZING: "Amazing New DVD Lowers Your Blood Pressure by Just Watching It!"

18. DO YOU: "Do You Know How to Stop Vicious Dog Attacks with the Push of a Button?"

19. WOULD YOU: "Would You Trade $2 for Our Famous Brick-Oven Pizza?"

20. CAN YOU: "Can You Be Sure Your Child Won't Get Kidnapped?"
21. IF YOU: "If You Hate Cleaning Your Pool, This Ad Brings Good News!"
22. STARTING TODAY: "Starting Today You Can Dance 97% Better...*If* You Follow These Rules."

Ad-Agency Secret #6: 12 Ways to Lure Readers Into Your Copy

You've written a great headline that targets your prospects and compels them to read more. You've briefly captured their attention, stirred their curiosity, and tapped their desires. *You don't want to lose them now!* But how do you start writing the body copy in a way that flows naturally from your headline and doesn't jar them out of this coveted—and potentially profitable—state of mind? Here are 12 easy ways to do it, based on successful results from hundreds of business-winning print ads.

Each of the following 12 examples uses the *same* headline as a springboard for our variations. The headline is:

"Just Released! Psychologist's Study Reveals Little-Known Speaking Patterns That Immediately Put Rude Salespeople in Their Place."

1. Continue the Thought in the Headline:

"You know the rude salespeople we mean. The ones with the big mouths who don't understand the word *no*. The ones who push and push and won't leave you alone...."

2. Ask a Question:

"How would *you* handle yourself in a sticky situation like this?"

3. Quote a Respected Authority:

"According to communication psychologist R. Butler Sinclair, there's no need for anyone to feel intimidated by the high-pressure tactics used by...."

4. Give 'Em a Free Taste:

"The next time you're confronted by a pushy salesperson, do this: Wait until he is finished speaking. Then raise your left hand to your mouth and say, 'You know, you really didn't....'"

5. Challenge Them to Prove It Works:

"Here's what we want you to do. Read pages 8 and 9 of this incredible new book—no more. Then go to the dealership with the reputation for the most obnoxious and belligerent...."

6. Start With a Story of Skepticism:

"When we first received the manuscript from the author, we were skeptical. But some of us in the editorial office actually tried some of Sinclair's tricks, and we were absolutely blown away."

7. Tell What Others Are Saying (Bandwagon Effect):

"Nobody hates obnoxious salespeople more than I do. So when I first saw the ad for this book I though it was too good to be true. It is, in fact, the most powerful book I've ever read on dealing with rude coworkers, salespeople, and mothers-in-law. —Bob Manstreth, Philadelphia, Pa."

8. Play Reporter:

"Philadelphia, PA—A New York psychologist has just released the findings of a seven-year study that explains how any man or woman can use the power of a new type of communication psychology to deal with obnoxious people."

9. Get Personal With You, You, You:

"Have *you* ever been hassled by a salesperson who can't take no for an answer? Do you hate when people push you around and manipulate you? Would you like to know a powerful new way to instantly put these obnoxious people in their place? A way that gives you the upper hand...."

10. Tell a Dramatic Story:

"According to communication psychologist R. Butler Sinclair, there's no longer any need for anyone to feel intimidated by the high-pressure tactics used by...."

11. Give Super-Detailed Specs:

"This amazing new book—a hefty 8 1/2 × 11-inch leather-bound, hardcover beauty—is jam-packed with over 327 pages, 10 information-filled chapters, and 45 of the most effective new communication tools ever developed for...."

12. Lure them with a Very Short First Sentence:

"Don't you hate it?"

"It's so annoying!"

"It makes me sick."

"I can't stand it!"

Ad-Agency Secret #7: 360 Degrees of Attention-Getting Power

Imagine a police lineup of 10 thugs. They're dressed like thugs. They have angry thug expressions. Scary thug teeth. Lousy thug shaving habits. And an overall aura of "thugosity." Standing in the middle of these upstanding citizens is a dapper gentleman that looks like he just stepped off his Gulfstream G550 private jet. Wow, does this guy look wealthy, or what? That suit! Those shoes! That million-dollar smile!

Question: Who stands out in the police lineup? Differences attract. "In a litter of 10 puppies, the purple pooch gets all the attention."

Thugs and puppies aside, in advertising we know that one way to get people's attention is via graphic design. Our goal isn't to make our advertising look the way everyone else's does. We want to stand out, don't we? But how many advertisers actually do? *Very* few. Prove it to yourself. Stop reading for a moment and grab your local newspaper. What shape are most ads? Without ever seeing the paper you're reading, I know that most are square, followed by rectangle. Over and over, and over...the same two shapes. Not because that's what's proven to be most effective. (It hasn't.) But simply because these shapes allow publishers to optimize their sales space. It's easy to fit them side by side.

So be a rebel, break away from the copycat pack, stand out on even the most crowded newspaper pages by running an eye-grabbing *circle* ad. The advertising industry publication *Printer's Ink* reported the effectiveness of this simple technique decades ago, but few advertisers know about it, and even fewer have ever used it. Instead of the typical rectangle or square, have your ad set within a circular border. (Run your copy the standard way; don't curve it around the interior of the circle.) Circular ads get more attention and yours will stand out—dramatically—from your "square" competition.

Simply ask your printer or newspaper (or better still, a graphic designer) to set your copy in a circular border that fits into the square ad space size you're buying. To emphasize the circle even more, fill with black—or the color of your choice—everything from the outside edge of the circle, all the way to the inside edges of the square that contains it. This leaves you with the entire inside of the circle for your copy. Because of its shape, you'll naturally have more horizontal room in the exact center of the circle than you will at the top and bottom. It's a real eye-catcher. And I don't care how many other ads your ad is surrounded by, yours will stick out like a neon sign in a sea of sameness.

> Successful small-space ads exploited their unusual shapes to enhance the depiction of the product. Poor ones tried to pack too much information into their ads and too little attention was paid to drawing in the reader in the first place.
> —"Great Newspaper Ads," *Marketing Magazine*, February 5, 2001

Ad-Agency Secret #8: The Reverse-Type Pitfall

"Oh no! Don't reverse it! Stop! Don't you dare print white letters on a dark background!"

You may have heard this one, from graphic designers, copywriters, creative directors, consultants, newspaper ad-sales reps, and other knowledgeable advertising people. But have you ever asked them, "Why not?" Chances are, they'll tell you, "It's harder to read," and nothing further.

Have you followed this advice? You should. Because the principle is grounded in sound psychological principle and fact. How about your Website? Your HTML ads? Your printed materials?

This no-no is called *reversing* or *knocking out* type. Unless your ad is surrounded, literally crammed by other ads on a Website, newspaper page, or anywhere else, don't do it. Studies show that reversing makes your copy dramatically less readable. Why?

Because the eye is not accustomed to reading in reverse. Especially if the type is small. Unfortunately, I've seen everyone from tiny family shops to giant corporations make this blunder. How many Websites have you seen on which the background is darker than the type? Very difficult to read.

Exception to the rule? Reversing out of a *solid* background *can* be effective with headlines when the type is large and the words are few; for example: "Free Chocolate Truffles!" or "Win This New Lamborghini!" Then again, you could probably print *those* headlines in yellow ink on white paper and they'd probably pull like crazy. But what's the background of this long-repeated admonishment? Rather than just tell you not to do it, you should understand *why* advertising professionals give you this advice...even though most of them have no idea themselves.

Experiment #1:
Mr. Holmes and His "Critical Sixty-Six"

In an article entitled "The Relative Legibility of Black Print and White Print," published in the *Journal of Applied Psychology* in 1931, a researcher by the mysterious name of G. Holmes performed a test using short words. Some words were printed in black ink on white paper, and others in white type on a black background. The same font and type size was used for all words. Good ol' Mr. Holmes displayed both words at a distance, far enough away so that his subjects could not read them. He then said, in effect, "OK gang, move forward only as close as necessary to read these words."

His findings? G. discovered that words set black on white (not reversed) could be read at a distance of about 66 inches, whereas the white on black (reversed) words could not be read until the subjects were closer, approximately 55 inches. Bottom line? *Reversing makes type less legible.*

Experiment #2:
Daniel Starch and the Eyeball Slowdown

Our advertising researcher friend Daniel Starch performed an experiment that agreed with Holmes's findings. Starch had participants read a short, non-reversed passage. "Read this!" he barked. In fact, the average participant read it at just faster than six words per second. Next, he had them read a passage printed in reverse. The speed? Just faster than four words per second, about two words per second *slower* than non-reversed printing. Bottom line? *Reversing slows down reading.*

Experiment #3:
When P&T Speak, Everyone Listens

It was time to bring in the top guns and get to the bottom of this whole reverse-type issue. And in they came: two psychologists, Paterson and Tinker. The big dogs of advertising research. Wasting no time, they repeated Starch's experiment, but with a twist that produced interesting results. When participants were shown the black-on-white version and were then immediately shown the reversed version, the reversed passage was proven to be 4 percent less legible. When they were only shown the reversed copy, it proved 16 percent less legible...statistically significant in anyone's book.

Verdict? Don't reverse it. Now you won't just be following advice like a mindless robot. You'll know *why* you're not doing it. Go ahead...enlighten your favorite advertising expert with this info. He or she may never look at you the same way again.

Ad-Agency Secret #9: Crush Your Competition With Extreme Specificity

This one idea is so powerful, it can help you establish a stranglehold on your competition. Its effectiveness has been hailed by legendary advertising masters, from the venerable Claude Hopkins ("Scientific Advertising") to the brilliant Eugene Schwartz ("Breakthrough Advertising").

I call it *extreme specificity*, and your competitors will curse you for it. It's simple, and here's what you do: From this day on, start being extremely specific every time you describe your products or services. Here's what I mean...

One day I conducted an experiment. I grabbed my telephone and the Yellow Pages. I called about 25 local pizza shops at random. I said: "Hello, I'm coming in with 10 friends this Saturday. I want to come to your place, but one of the guys wants to go to another pizzeria. Help me convince the group; what makes your pizza better?"

Call #1 Response: [Annoyed] "Uhhh...I don't know. That's for YOU to decide!"

Analysis: Pathetic. Here's a guy who was given the opportunity by a cash-wielding customer to distinguish his restaurant from the rest. In 30 seconds, he could have won up to 10 new customers for many years.

Call #2 Response: "We use better ingredients."

Analysis: This reply tells me nothing. It creates no positive images in my mind, and gives me no reason to desire *his* pizza. The response is too generic. Another chance to stand out from the crowd, blown.

Call #3 Response: "Better quality. Our sauce and flour are from Italy."

Analysis: Not great, but better! He doesn't just say "quality," or "ingredients," but he also specifies *which* ingredients. Then he says they're better because they're true *Italian* ingredients. It sure sounds better than flour and cheese made in the Bronx.

But could he have done better? Absolutely. How about telling me what makes the cheese better, that's it's not just cow-milk mozzarella, but also incredibly flavorful (and hard-to-find) buffalo milk mozzarella, and according to true New York style tradition, the cheese is never shredded, but placed on top in *chunks* because shredded cheese releases too much moisture on the pie.

The flour? Only hard, northern spring wheat because of its excellent rising qualities, crisp exterior, and chewy interior crust. But why stop there? His sauce...ahhhh, now's *this* is a thing of beauty. He refuses to use pre-prepared sauce (like his competitors), no sir. He crushes his own tomatoes. (And not any old tomatoes, either. He insists on "Genuine San Marzano" tomatoes from Italy!) Olive oil? Only extra-virgin Olivieri, of course. The dough is hand-stretched—not flatted by steel rollers in a mindless machine like those big-chain guys. His pizza masterpieces are baked in a coal-burning oven imported directly from Italy, which imparts an amazing flavor, unmatched by the competition's plain old gas ovens.

Meats and vegetables? His competitors use pre-processed ingredients, delivered in giant, institutional-size poly bags. Here, everything is hand-sliced fresh every morning. Herbs? He grows fresh basil and oregano for maximum flavor. And talk about atmosphere! His cozy dining room was recently renovated floor-to-ceiling, nearly doubled in size, and with his big new booths, it's far more comfortable than most other pizza shops' cheap plastic chairs. Look at that gorgeous Italian tile and fabulous artwork. As if all *that* wasn't enough, his family has been handcrafting pizza for four generations. You taste 80 years of pizza-baking mastery with every crispy bite.

"But Drew! Does any of this really matter in today's "charge-the-consumer-more-and-give him-less" world?" Yes. It matters more than ever, especially because no one else is doing it. One of the most powerful things you can do is educate your prospects about the specifics of your product or service. Once educated—assuming your product is at least as good as the competition—they'll better appreciate what you're offering. Think...what interesting story can *you* tell people about your product or service? How can you educate them about what you do or how you do it?

A Tale of Two Restaurants

Restaurant #1, Luigi's, tells you it has wonderful home cooking. Chicken parmesan, spaghetti, manicotti, and more. Plus, a coupon. Yes, that's the *entire* ad. Gee guys, the idea in advertising is to stand out, differentiate yourself, and persuade people to take action. I give Luigi's credit for the coupon, but the rest of the ad doesn't give any compelling reasons to redeem it.

Now let's look at Restaurant #2, Fratelli's. Similar to Luigi's, they list what they serve. They also give a coupon. But they do much more, by giving extreme specifics about their food. They differentiate themselves in the marketplace by saying things people want to know:

"We make our bread fresh every day, golden and crusty. Our pasta is made from scratch. We use only fresh herbs in all our recipes. Only pure, cold-pressed 100-percent virgin olive oil is served. Spring water fills your glass, mellow Italian music fills the air, and softly glowing candles light your table."

Wow! Can you feel the difference? Yes...it's actually a *feeling*. You get a better feeling for Fratelli's. The ad tells you more. It's not just trying to sell you. It's actually wooing you. The words put pictures in your head and cause you to demonstrate the food and atmosphere in your head long before you step through the door.

How many restaurants go this far to educate you about what they do? Even if every other restaurant in the city does the same exact thing, because no one else is saying it, the one who does say it, wins! So ask yourself: "What can I say about my product or service that may be obvious to me, but my market knows little about? Can I tell them about the processes used, the time, money, and effort expended? How can I point out the major advantages of my product and make people begin to question the quality of my competition?"

Here's how another business uses this technique.

A Tale of Two Hardware Stores

What do most independent hardware stores do in their ads? Very little. They're often no more than business cards with a quick mention of the few items they have on sale. Consider the copy from the following two ads.

Hardware Store #1:

Hammers, screwdrivers, power tools, home fix-up, lawn and garden equipment. Paulson's has the hardware you're looking for...at neighborhood-friendly prices!

Hardware Store #2:

Handyman Jack's is no ordinary hardware store. We're a Hardware Super Store! We carry 343 kinds of fasteners, 28 types of nails, 86 gauges of wire, 43 grit sizes of sandpaper, 16 different styles of hammers, 28 kinds of screwdrivers, 47 types of keys, a daily inventory of 354,000 bolts and screws, all the top-name power tools for less, and a no-nonsense, money-back guarantee of complete satisfaction.

Question: If you needed hardware and you knew nothing about either of these stores except what you saw in the ad, and both stores were about the same distance from your home...where would you go? The answer is obvious: Handyman Jack's. Even if every other hardware store in the city carries the same exact merchandise, no one else says it.

Remember: It's not important that people *need* to know all that information. I mean, who really cares how many nails and bolts you have, as long as you have what they want. But the psychology behind it—the Length-Implies-Strength heuristic—makes it tremendously potent. Because hardly any other store says these things, people judge the one who *does* say it to be better, more complete, more successful in some way. Don't you want to convey that?

Ad-Agency Secret #10:
The Famous Ogilvy Layout Principle

Often called "The Father of Advertising," ad agency genius David Ogilvy created some of the best-known ads of his day. He developed a simple layout formula that, if followed, results in eye-catching ads that win researcher Daniel Starch's "most-noted award." Called the Two-Thirds/One-Third Principle—or, more affectionately, the "Ogilvy"— the top two thirds of the ad is one big photograph. The remaining third of the ad consists of the headline (directly under the photo) and the sales copy beneath the headline, often starting with a large "drop cap"— just as I did in this paragraph—to help lure readers' eyes into your sales message. Your company logo tucks neatly into the lower-right corner.

> If you start your body copy with a drop-initial, you increase readership by an average of 13%.
>
> —David Ogilvy

There's also the Reverse Ogilvy—the One-Third/Two-Thirds variation, wherein the top third of the ad is a photo, a headline underneath it, and the remaining two thirds is sales copy. As before, you drop your company logo in the lower-right corner. In both cases, the headline and body copy become, in effect, a "caption" for the photo.

> Place the headline under the visual, as the eye moves to the picture first and then moves down.
>
> —Starch Research

Unless you know the following fact, you may not appreciate just how clever this layout is. *Studies show that up to twice as many people read captions as body copy.* Ogilvy himself advised, "More people read the captions under illustrations than read the body copy, so never use an illustration without putting a caption under it." It's a clever trick that's stood the test of time and has helped many big companies become leaders in their respective industries. If it's good enough for "The man in the Hathaway shirt" and Rolls-Royce, it's likely good enough for you and me.

Don't run pictures without putting captions under them.
Put a brief selling message or human interest message
under every illustration you use.

—John Caples

Ad-Agency Secret #11:
The Psychology of Typefaces

Typefaces can be playful. Authoritative. Creative. Beautiful. Dramatic. Fancy. Odd. Refined. And yes, even downright hideous. And because of this, different typefaces can color our messages with different meanings. For example, you wouldn't advertise frilly women's lingerie using a headline set in dark, bold, and masculine Cooper Black. On the other hand, you wouldn't advertise your hardcore bodybuilding gym packed with sweaty and grunting steroid-injecting monsters using Palace, a lovely, delicate, and wispy script font. Your ad would look ridiculous! Of course, *your* product may not suggest a typeface that's so categorically expressive of any particular emotion or visual, but no matter what typestyle you choose, just know that it *will* communicate *something*.

It is possible to blow away three-quarters
of our readers simply by choosing the wrong
type. If you rely on words to sell, that should
concern you deeply.

—Colin Wheildon, author of *Type & Layout: Are You
Communicating or Just Making Pretty Shapes?*

In addition to dozens of studies done in the past few decades, several recent tests have been conducted to determine which typestyles are easiest to read. I've heard a few people say, "Whatever you're used to reading is what's easiest for you."

Hogwash! Of course some typefaces are easier to read than others; it's ridiculous to say otherwise. Still, you can get *used* to scrubbing your dirty clothes on a rock, but that doesn't mean that pressing "start" on your washing machine isn't easier.

Consider the typeface called Flag Day. Each letter looks like a little waving flag consisting of alternating and undulating horizontal black and white stripes. It's one of the most difficult-to-read typefaces I've seen. At 24 points and under, I can't read it. Larger than 24 points, I *still* can't read it. Even when I type my own name, I might as well have typed the random words "Spinning Flounder Ape." Now, I don't care how many typeface studies you conducted, the fact is, Flag Day is extremely difficult to read because the letters simply don't look like letters, but wiggly striped blobs. I'm sure you *could* get used to it. But that doesn't mean that a clearer, plainer font such as Arial wouldn't be far more readable. Saying otherwise is like saying, "Heck, I've been using the same dull razor blade for 28 years...using a brand new one wouldn't be any easier; I'm already used to the old dull one!" Huh?

Serif or Sans Serif for Printed Matter?

Do you know the difference between a serif and a sans serif typeface? Your eye certainly does. A serif typeface is one that has little feet and embellishments on the tips and base of each letter, such as this font. Sans (the French word "without") serif faces, such as this font, have no such serifs. The serifs make each letter more distinct and recognizable.

Multiple researchers confirm that serif fonts make words easier to read. (Wordon, 1991; Hartley, 1994). Examples of serif fonts are Times New Roman, Palatino, Schoolbook, Georgia, Courier, Cheltenham, Bookman, and Garamond.

In 1926, The British Medical Council reported that sans serif type causes *irradiation*: an optical anomaly in which space between lines intruded into letters, creating a type of light-vibration that made reading more difficult and uncomfortable.

In a study of comprehension, Wheildon (1986) noted that only 12 percent of participants effectively comprehended a passage set in sans serif type, versus 67 percent of readers given a version set in a serif typeface. Those given the sans serif version said they had a tough time reading the text and had to "continually back-track to regain comprehension."

In a substantial test of several hundred thousand readers, Wheildon set one ad in three different faces: Garamond, Times Roman (both serif), and Helvetica (sans serif). Here's what he found:

* Garamond was read and comprehended by 670,000 people—66 percent of the test subjects.
* Times Roman was comprehended by 320,000—less than half of Garamond.
* Helvetica was comprehended by only 120,000 people— 12.5 percent of the subjects.

Bottom line: Serif fonts—at least on paper—are simply easier to read. The findings are the same for virtually every researcher who's ever conducted the test. No wonder most newspaper and magazine publishers set their body copy in a serif typeface.

"Okay Drew, I get it, but which *specific* serif typeface should I use?" Ahhh, now *that* question opens an entirely new can of worms. Unfortunately, I've seen no research that gives a definitive answer. And my studies go back as far as 1912—yikes!—when B.E. Roethlin wrote the article, "The Relative Legibility of Different Typefaces of Printing Types," in the *American Journal of Psychology*. (Good luck Googling that!)

The closest was a study by Paterson and Tinker (1932) that revealed no discernable differences in reading speed among the group of faces they studied, with the exception of two styles that slowed readers: Cloister Black (Old English), by 16.5 percent, and American Typewriter, by 5.1 percent.

That's not to say that people don't have their opinions.

John McWade, publisher of *Before & After* magazine, likes: Adobe Caslon, Adobe Garamond, ITC Stone Serif, and Janson Text 55 Roman.

Coauthors James Craig, Irene Korol Scala, and William Bevington, of *Designing With Type: The Essential Guide to Typography*, say, "Baskerville is considered one of the most pleasant and readable typefaces."

Advertising copy great John Caples liked using Cheltenham Bold for headlines.

David Ogilvy preferred the Century family, Caslon, Baskerville, and Jenson.

Direct marketing guru Gary Halbert swore by Courier for sales letters.

Yours truly often uses Clearface Black for headlines and Schoolbook for body copy.

Ascender Corporation's study "Fonts on the Front Page" revealed the 10 most popular typefaces used by the top 100 U.S newspapers (by circulation), in order:

1. Poynter Series.
2. Franklin Gothic.
3. Helvetica.
4. Utopia.
5. Times.
6. Nimrod.
7. Century Old Style.
8. Interstate.
9. Bureau Grotesque.
10. Miller.

Until research says otherwise, using any of the serif fonts suggested here will not only put you in good company, but will also help you create attractive, more readable sales materials.

Set Headlines in Initial Caps

Headlines Longer Than Just a Couple of Words, Such As **"FREE COOKIES!"** Should Be Set in *Initial Caps*, a Combination of Upper- and Lower-Case Letters, As in This Sentence. All upper-case letters slowed readership by 11.8 percent (Paterson and Tinker, 1956).

New York Times editor Theodore Bernstein challenged Paterson and Tinker's findings and said headlines set in *all* caps could be read faster. The battle raged. And when the smoke cleared, poor Mr. Bernstein ate his caps.

Results: An 18.9 percent difference in favor of initial cap headlines—even greater than Paterson and Tinker found in *their* study. Gulp.

But wait! Tinker wasn't done. He was so fascinated by this whole caps/lower case issue that he conducted a test to see if how much a person blinked—yes, *blinked*—could be a reliable measure of readability (Tinker, 1946).

Results: All capital letters slowed reading—no surprise there—but he struck no gold with his eyelid-driven "blinky-blink" hypothesis.

But *why* do all caps slow reading? Because the eye recognizes by *outline*.

Try this test: Draw a line around the following two words: ADVER-TISING POWER, allowing your pen to touch the tops and bottoms of each letter. The resultant shape is a rectangle, with even sides all around. Now draw a line around the following two words set in initial caps, again allowing your pen to touch the tops and bottoms of each letter: Advertising Power. Your pen rises and falls like a roller coaster as it goes over the capital letters and the ascenders and descenders of the other letters.

Results: More distinct and recognizable letters and words. This translates into easier and faster reading.

Serif or Sans Serif for Online Reading?

What looks good on paper doesn't necessarily read well on screen. The difference? Resolution. For example, books, newspapers, flyers, and brochures are typically printed in 300 dots-per-inch (dpi) resolution. If you have a Mac (or MacOS compatible), you have a 72 dpi screen. If you have a Windows PC, you have a 96 dpi screen. What looks good in one medium doesn't look great in another.

Google the topic, and you'll discover more online font readability tests than you'd believe *anyone* had interest in. I'll share the bottom-line results of a few of them, and then give you a recommendation that considers *all* the findings.

Some researchers used proofreading to determine readability, such as Tullis, Boynton, & Hersh in 1995 for their study for Fidelity Investments. They looked at 12 different fonts in sizes from 6 to 9.75 points.

Results: The most preferred fonts were Arial and MS Sans Serif at 9.75 points.

Two other researchers (Bernard and Mills, 2000) evaluated 10- and 12-point Arial and Times New Roman fonts.

Results: No reliable differences in reading speed or in error detection. However, the readers said they *preferred* the 12-point fonts.

Bernard didn't stop there. He put three different font sizes (10, 12, and 14 points) in eight different typefaces on the chopping block (Bernard, et al., 2001)— four serif fonts: Century Schoolbook, Courier New, Georgia, and Times New Roman, and four sans serif fonts: Arial, Comic Sans, Tahoma, and Verdana.

Results:

1. Subjects read Arial and Times New Roman faster than Courier, Schoolbook, and Georgia.

115

2. Subjects read the 12-point fonts faster than the 10-point fonts.

3. Subjects preferred all the fonts—except Century Schoolbook—over Times New Roman.

In 2002, the Software Usability Research Laboratory published the results of a study titled "A Comparison of Popular Online Fonts: Which Size and Type is Best?"

Results:

1. The most legible fonts were Arial, Courier, and Verdana.

2. At 10 points, participants preferred Verdana. Times New Roman was the least preferred.

3. At 12 points, Arial was preferred and Times New Roman the least preferred.

4. The preferred font overall was Verdana, and Times New Roman was the least preferred.

Bottom line: For easiest online reading, use Arial for 12-point text and larger. Smaller than 12 point? Verdana, but rarely go smaller than 10 point. For a more formal look, use Georgia. For older readers, use 14 point.

CA$HVERTISING Tip: Set long headlines in black. Other colors—yes, even red—are more difficult to read. White backgrounds are best, followed by yellow. And just as with hardcopy printing, avoid reversing text, as discussed in Ad Agency Secret #8: The Reverse-Type Pitfall.

Ad-Agency Secret #12:
Insist on the Pro-Design Difference

Owning a hammer doesn't make you a carpenter. Having a scalpel doesn't make you a doctor. And using graphic design software does *not* make you a graphic designer. So, I beg you, don't design your own sales materials. I've seen ads that were so amateurish they looked as though they were designed by Miss Susan's Romper Room class. Your image is critical—especially when promoting to those who don't know you. Many sales are won and lost simply by how you graphically represent yourself.

CA$HVERTISING Tip: Call some local ad agencies, ask to speak to the art or creative director, and say, "Hello, my name is [your name here] and I'm hoping you could help me. I run a small business and

I'm putting together an [ad, brochure, flyer]. Could you recommend a good freelance designer?" They usually work with several, so ask for a few. Or, if you choose to find a designer online, be sure to review his or her portfolio. Ask how much he or she charges, and whether he or she bills hourly or per project. Some are expensive, some not. Many charge depending upon how big a company they think you are. (Hint: don't sound big.) Or, if money's tight, call local graphic arts schools. They can usually recommended students who'd be thrilled to do the job cheaply. But before spending a penny, ask for samples. Some will be great; others will make you run away in horror.

Ad-Agency Secret #13: The Power of Questions

What kind of questions? Any kind! Just look at the writing in this book. You'll see many examples of this ploy. *What does it do?* (The last sentence is a perfect example.) It causes your prospects to desire the answer. *So what happens?* They continue reading to find out the answer. I love this technique. *Why?* Because it works like a lure to help me capture greater readership. Use it in headlines. Use it in subheads. And of course, us it in your body copy.

According to neuro-linguistic programming (NLP) proponents, questions create what's called an *open loop* in the reader's brain. *Want an example?* (Note the open loop I just created.) *Do you want to know one simple technique that will triple your coupon response with no additional cost or effort?* Did you catch your own response? If you're similar to most other businesspeople, you probably responded (at least internally) with a yes. Because you want to know the answer to that question, I have effectively "installed" an open loop in your brain.

The hypothesis is that once the open loop is installed, the brain will continue to search for information in order to close the loop. And although I've seen no scientific research to support that claim, questions *are* a powerful way to keep people reading. I know a business trainer who uses this technique. Instead of just rambling, he continually inserts questions into his talks. Every question grabs his audience's attention and challenges them to answer it. Asking questions keeps everyone alert because it acts like mini "pop quizzes that help keep listeners on their toes."

So now that I've revealed this little ploy, be alert to how I use it in this book, okay? Notice how it affects you and how it turns what would otherwise be a monologue into something that feels more like a two-way conversation.

Ad-Agency Secret #14:
The "Granny Rule" of Direct Mail

Let's say you're face-to-face with a salesman named Larry. Larry sells seafood. (And he smells like it too.) Today Larry would like to sell you lobsters, and he thinks you'll be a darn good prospect.

First, Larry will try to establish rapport with you. According to the American Heritage Dictionary, rapport is "a relationship of mutual trust or emotional affinity." In other words, Larry wants you to like him. That way, you'll be more likely to buy his big ol' lobsters.

To influence you to like him, Larry will "meet you in your world" by talking about things to which you can relate. If you like cars, he'll talk about the gorgeous new Lexus LF-A Roadster. If you like Mexican food, he'll tell you about Las Palomas, a cozy little restaurant on the water-front in Puerto Vallarta that makes killer margaritas the size of your head. If you like dogs, he'll show you a picture of his adorable flat-coated retriever, Joey. If Larry does everything right, you'll begin to think that Larry is a lot like you. Larry, therefore, has succeeded in establishing rapport. You're now more likely to accept what he says, and buy what he sells. (Sound familiar? It's Consumer Psychology Principle #10—the Cialdini *Liking* cue.)

After a bunch of preliminary yakking, Larry will eventually open his briefcase and pull out all kinds of samples to further entice you to buy his freshly caught—and still snappin'—lobsters.

Now, let's make an analogy. *Sales letters* are like Larry's words. They're personal, one-on-one, and try to "meet you in your world." *Brochures*, by contrast, are like Larry's briefcase: impersonal, and filled with samples, photos, and complete details. Each component works in a different way for the same end result: the sale.

Remember: Advertising is a salesperson in print, a salesperson broadcasted to the masses.

Your sales letter is your salesperson. Think of it that way! It should be personal. A good salesperson wouldn't greet you by saying, "Hello, Occupant...," and neither should your sales letter. It should meet your prospects in their world. Suppose you're mailing to teenagers (big spenders!), don't say:

> Dear Justin:
>
> The weekend is young and most of your friends have already made plans well in advance. You, however, sit at home staring at the telephone.

Instead, say:

> Hey Justin...
>
> If you're sick and tired of staying home every weekend doing nothing but surfing the Web when all your friends are out partying up a storm...

Do you feel the difference? It's actually a feeling! It's more positive, upbeat, youthful, exciting, and personal. A good salesperson doesn't talk like a robot:

> It is recommended that you act promptly regardless of the nature of your present dating situation.

UGH! Instead, a good salesperson talks like a human being:

> Hey Justin, haven't you had your eye on that hottie long enough? Aren't you sick of just sitting back and letting every other guy with more guts ask her out? Come on, try my Instant Confidence System...if it doesn't work, I'll return your money by PayPal within 48 hours. What could be fairer?

The best way to write any advertising is to start by making a list of all the benefits your product or service offers. So go ahead, write them down. Don't just say, "Yeah, yeah. I don't feel like writing them down—I know what the benefits are in my head." Do it! And remember: Write only the benefits, not the features. (Refer to Ad Agency Secret #2: Bombard Your Readers with Benefits for a quick refresher.) After you've completed your list, rank them in order of importance—to your *customer*, not to you. That is, list the benefit you feel is the strongest selling point as #1, and so on, down the list. When you're done, you'll have a list of the key selling points of your product.

Now take the #1 benefit and work that benefit into the *opening* of your letter.

CA$HVERTISING Tip: It's always a good idea to work the idea of ease and quickness into your first sentence. That's because we live in a quick-fix society. People want ease and speed. If what you offer lends itself to these appeals, then use them! For example:

Do you want a fast, easy way to coax your car to get 22 percent better gas mileage?

Do you want a fast way to pack on 20 pounds of lean muscle without heavy weight training or crazy dieting?

Would you like to know a simple, 5-minute trick that guarantees to improve your memory, or double your money back?

Do you know about the FBI-tested interrogation technique that instantly reveals if someone is lying to you?

Whether you're sending an e-mail or a hardcopy letter, your salutation is most effective when it's personalized. "Dear Bob" is always better than "Dear Friend." When you can't personalize, try using a salutation that connotes how your prospect will change after buying your product: "Dear Weekend Warrior," or "Dear Soon-to-Be-Millionaire." And please, never ever say "Dear Occupant"! You'd slam the door in my face if I came to your house with that "powerful" opener.

CA$HVERTISING Tip: Start your letter with a question. It's an extremely effective device for getting people to read deeper.

Remember: The purpose of your *first* sentence and paragraph is to get people to read your *second* sentence and paragraph. And so on. Keep this in mind when you write so that your sentences flow smoothly into each other, like hot fudge over creamy French vanilla custard.

Now, back to our opening sentence. Asking a question in your first sentence—especially one that starts, **"Do you want...?"**—and following it with an extremely positive benefit, is a great way to keep your prospect reading.

Do you want to know the secret of making killer FAT-FREE cheesecake?

Do you know how to buy LUXURY real estate for 50% off market value?

Do you know the secret of getting FREE yoga lessons in your area?

Do you want to DOUBLE, even TRIPLE your reading speed in 3 days?

Do you see the power of these simple questions? What you're doing is simply asking your prospects if they want the benefit that your product gives them.

Tough talk: People expect that 99 percent of their mail will be trash. In fact, many people open their mail over a trash can. You have only seconds to grab their attention and stir their interest...or lose them forever.

AIDA to the Rescue

Most everyone knows the AIDA formula. It's an age-old method of structuring the elements of your sales message in a certain, predetermined order. It stands for Attention, Interest, Desire, Action. It says that your #1 job is to grab people's *attention*. Then you build *interest*. Next you stimulate *desire*. And finally you push your reader to take *action*.

Say, for example, that you discovered the cure for cancer. You excitedly write to the FDA to announce the good news. Assuming you didn't know the AIDA technique, you shove your letter into an envelope that looks like the thousands of other envelopes the FDA gets every day. Imagine...they'll probably open their electric bill before your letter about the cure for cancer! No good. You need to somehow make your envelope stand out from the others.

Do you know how to tease?

The message on your outside envelope (called the "OSE" or "carrier" in agency circles) is referred to as the "teaser." The teaser can either give information about your offer or be totally non-content-specific. In my opinion, you should rarely use informational teasers on your OSE unless your product is pin-point targeted to your mailing list—and hopefully it is. Why? Because teasers immediately tell the recipient that the envelope contains a sales pitch. I'd much rather use nonspecific teasers such as, "PERSONAL ATTENTION OF:," "PERSONAL LETTER FOR:," or "IMPORTANT LETTER FOR:" typed above the addressee's name and address, if anything at all.

Try these tips

Try brightly colored envelopes. Rubberstamp or print the word, "URGENT" in bloodred ink. Use lots of stamps of smaller denominations on the front, rather than just one stamp. And here's a great trick I use after fulfilling an information request from someone who called me on the phone: Write a personal message on the front of the envelope, next to their typewritten name and address, such as: "Eileen: Here's the Information We Talked About! —Drew."

But what if you've had no phone contact, you're mailing to a non-specific audience, and they haven't even requested what you're sending? Well, how about, "Mirko: Please Read This Letter Before 9:30 Tonight! —Drew." (Then justify the 9:30 deadline in the letter somehow, as in, it's an ordering deadline or the like.) Or "Cyndi: Please Tell Me if I'm Wrong About You —Drew." The variations are endless.

These personal teasers work best with a personal-looking OSE, something that looks as though an individual—not a corporation—created it either by hand, or with one's personal ink-jet printer.

And now, back to our story...

After opening your envelope, the folks at the FDA will next pull out your letter. If you didn't know that your #1 job of *each* of your components (OSE, letter, brochure, and so on) is to first get attention, you might destroy your letter's effectiveness by grinding out some boring nonsense that sounds as though you're applying for a job:

Dear Mr. Manstreth:

For the past 23 years I have worked for some of the most forward-thinking medical labs in the country. From New York to California, I have worked for the Kennedy Institute, the Sinclair Research Center, the Rosen Clinic, and the Lawrence Biology Lab. In all that time, I dreamed of one day being able to write you this letter. Under the enormous funding of blah, blah, blah...

Yawn! What's this guy's problem? He discovered the cure for cancer and he's boring his reader with the energy-sapping details of his career path? He *should* have FedExed it or sent a Western Union telegram for the urgent look it deserves. Next, he should have scrapped all that boring career fluff and gotten right to the point!

Dear Mr. Manstreth:

I have discovered the cure for cancer.

I was informed by Eileen Axelrod to set an appointment to meet with both you and Scott Lawrence of your Investigation Center as soon as possible.

122

Enclosed are the preliminary details of my findings as well as my medical credentials.

Please call me immediately at (213) 123-4567.

Sincerely,

I.M. Rich

Like a hungry giant octopus, the first sentence grabs the reader's attention using only seven simple words! Of course, I realize that *your* product or service probably doesn't carry the same weight as the cure for cancer (no matter how good your return policy), so let's look at some others, shall we?

Start your sales letters this way

Let's say you sell a tear gas spray to women. The opening of your letter should *not* be:

Dear Janet,

In these days of uncertainty on our streets, we continually read about the horrors that women face. We read frightening statistics that paint a gloomy picture of blah blah blah...

Instead, write:

Dear Janet,

Can you protect yourself against a 220-pound rapist?

Which grabbed your attention? The answer's obvious!

Now, let's say you sell DVDs that teach people how to be more self-confident. Don't write:

Dear Eric,

Recent advances in brain-mind technology are so exciting! By simply playing a DVD, you can build self-confidence, boost self-esteem, blah blah blah...

Instead, write:

Dear Eric,

Would you like to DOUBLE, TRIPLE, even QUADRUPLE your self-confidence? If so, this letter will change your life.

Because in just 10 days from now, I'm going to give you the unshakable self-confidence of the most powerful business and military leaders of this century. Read on...

Question: If *you* wanted to be more self-confident, which letter opening would grab *your* attention? Again, it's obvious. So why don't more people write their advertising copy this way? Because they're too timid. They're afraid of offending people. They're more concerned with making their copy sound pretty, elegant, and graceful. Personally, I don't give a damn how graceful my copy sounds. I'm writing for response.

Fact: People aren't waiting for your offer to arrive, so there's no time for tippy toeing. You need to make a big impact *fast!*

The Granny Rule says that to grab people's attention with your direct mail, it helps to make your mailing like something your dear granny would send you. Imagine her, so sweet, covered with her multicolored, patchwork, hand-crocheted shawl, getting out a *plain, white* envelope. She grabs an ordinary *blue* ball point pen. And she *handwrites* your name and address. Then she grabs a piece of simple *white* paper and handwrites a letter to you, *calling you by name*, and writing the way grandmothers do: conversationally, warmly, with real concern for your well being (along with a precisely metered induction of guilt so you visit more often). She then licks the envelope, affixes a real live *postage stamp*, and mails it.

The fact is, the things Granny does are actually some of the most effective things any business can do when preparing a direct mailing—not slick; not expensive. But simple and personal. And you know what? Granny gets every one of her letters opened. Why? Because they look personal! About 99 percent of the mailings today look exactly like what they are: *solicitations*. They look as though they're screaming, "Hey Dumbo! Open this envelope fast! We're a big company that hired an expensive ad agency to create this mailing to shoe-horn open your wallet in 60 seconds flat!"

What a waste. Unless your mailing is so well-targeted (being mailed to people who have proven to, or are very likely to, be interested in the exact type of product or service you're selling), your slick package will most likely end up in the trash.

For example, I know that if I want to make money selling a weight-gain product to body builders, I'd look for a mailing list of bodybuilders who have purchased online or via mail order, and have bought recently, and frequently, and spent a lot of money. Anytime you buy a mailing list, the most important factors, after finding names that are likely to respond to your type of offer, are:

1. Recency of purchase (the more recent the better).
2. Frequency of purchase (the more times they bought your type of product the better).
3. High Dollar Amount Spent (this shows greater commitment than someone who spent just $2.50).

For example, if you can get a hotline list (folks who purchased very recently) of people who have bought similar products and have spent big bucks to do so, *and* have bought a number of times, then you have a potentially super list for your product.

Please don't use mailing labels to address your OSEs. It screams "MASS MAILING HERE!" Either buy a printer that lets you feed a stack of envelopes, or let a good letter shop spray the names in a realistic handwriting font. Or give the whole project to a senior citizens group and pay them to hand-address the envelopes. For just a few bucks you'll have the most appealing form of addressing. (Plus, you would have given a group of nice people an interesting job to do.) Handwriting grabs attention. They're the OSEs people usually tear into first. Why? Because they look like a personal letter from a dear old friend.

For the sales letter? Choose a nice, readable font. I used to swear by Courier because it looks so personal, and I still use it at times. But the definition of a "personal-looking" font is changing, with everyone now using serif fonts such as Times, Schoolbook, Bookman, and Palatino.

For the *response device* (what we ad-folk call the order form), a grandmotherly thing to do would be to never call it an "Order Form," but a "Personal Trial Certificate." Or "Personal, No-Obligation Trial Certificate." And if you can have your recipient's name and address already on this form, so much the better. Print it on a nice canary (yellow) paper so it stands out from the other pieces in the mailing. Always restate the offer on this piece. And use the big word "YES!" to the right of a square box with a bold check mark in it connoting approval.

Master John Caples advises to always show (on the form) a small picture of what people get when they reply. For example, if it's an order form for a book, *show* the book. Play up your guarantee too. Put your mailing address, phone number, and e-mail and Web addresses on the bottom of this form in case they lose the rest of your mailing. In fact, your name and address should appear on *all* of your components.

And remember the *scarcity* factor. Be sure you stress how urgent it is to return the form without delay. If you have a deadline to respond, great! Make sure it not only appears in your letter, brochure, and other materials, but also on your response device to give them an extra prod. Remember, without a deadline, people are inclined to just "think about it."

And lastly, include a BRE (business reply envelope) to take the last obstacle out of the responding process, should they choose not to order online. Hey, do you want to lose a sale because your prospect couldn't find a stamp, or was too lazy to address an envelope? You can even smack a real "live" stamp on a reply envelope if you don't have or wish to get a business reply permit. And because people all want ultra-fast service, use a little psychology by printing or rubberstamping in red, "RUSH! ORDER ENCLOSED!" or "24-HOUR PROCESSING" or some similar wording to give the reply envelope a more active, important look.

Now, go forth into the direct mail world like dear ol' Granny and, er, kick ass!

Ad-Agency Secret #15:
The Psychology of "Social Proof"

It doesn't matter if you sell to doctors or pizzeria owners; people believe testimonials. They have since the very first one was used in 1926 by Ponds, the cold-cream company. And if *you're* not using them, you're not just missing the boat, but the 220,000-ton Royal Caribbean *Oasis of the Seas*—the largest cruse ship on planet Earth!

How do you get them? Ask! Simply write a letter (or e-mail) to your customers and say, "We want to make you famous!" Then tell them you want their honest opinions about your product or service. Explain that you're putting together a new ad, brochure, Website, what have you, and you'd like to use their testimonial along with, if they'd like, their photo. In exchange for this, most folks will be happy with a few copies of the finished piece to show friends and family.

For example, let's say you're a Website designer. You might ask questions such as, "What do you think about our design services? What kind of response are you getting from your new site? How do our services compare with other designers you've used? What do you like best about the way we do business? Are our prices reasonable? Would you recommend us to a friend? Would you hire us again?"

Then, under the questions, I put a legal disclaimer that says, "I give Flaming Radish Web Design permission to use my quotes above, in complete or edited form, [ ] with/[ ] without my name and city/state (your address/phone number will not be used) for advertising/publicity purposes. As full compensation, Flaming Radish will provide me with 10 copies of the first printed piece in which my testimonial appears."

Simply provide a signature and date line, and that's it! It's so easy, it boggles my brain why more businesses aren't using testimonials. Remember to send the copies of the printed piece. These copies are what the law calls "consideration," which essentially binds the agreement. Or, if you'd prefer, send your request with $1.00. Say, "We're enclosing $1.00 to help cover any expenses you have in returning this form to us." In this case, the $1.00 becomes the consideration. And don't allow them to incur any expense in returning the form to you. *You* pay the return postage by means of a self-addressed stamped envelope (SASE).

Remember: If you want people to respond to your offer, you have to make it as easy as possible for them! Don't *you* be the lazy one!

Ad-Agency Secret #16:
The Guillotine Principle

I call this the "Guillotine Technique," and it's a proven eyeball-grabber. It's based on the notion that a head or face is the best attention-getter. Simply put a photo of someone's head in your ad. The face/head should be looking directly at the reader. Smiling is generally preferable, but of course this depends upon what type of product or service you're offering. The screaming, distorted face of a 235-pound mugger would be a real shocker in an ad for tear gas.

Are you a carpenter? Put a close-up of your face somewhere in your ad! A dentist? Show your face! Not only does a face attract immediate attention, but it gives your ad a warmer, more personal feel. Nothing fancy is needed. Even a tiny black-and-white photo will do.

The byproduct of all this is added trust, because now you're more than just a nameless (and faceless!) business; you're a real person. In addition, the constant repetition of your photo can make you famous. Include your face and name in all your ads, and you'll soon become a household word. (And possibly get stopped on the street every now and then: "Hey, aren't you...?")

CA$HVERTISING Tip: Put your photo at the top of your ad and make your headline a quote from you. For example, next to my photo in my ad, the headline reads (quote marks included), "Give Me 90 Minutes & I'll Show You How to Double...Triple...Quadruple Your Ad Response!" You can't help but notice it. So give the "guillotine" a go!

Ad-Agency Secret #17: PVAs—The Easy Way to Boost the Power of Your Copy

Question: Which of the following sentences conveys more excitement and interest to you?

1. You get six red apples hand-picked by my mother from our backyard farm, so delicious, they're probably the best apples you've ever eaten.

2. Just wait until you sink your teeth into the sweetest, juiciest, most mouth-watering Red Delicious apples you've ever eaten! Not just one or two. But a full one-dozen of these crisp, luscious beauties, each one carefully hand-picked by my 73-year old mother from the golden, sun-drenched orchards in our very own backyard!

The answer is obvious, isn't it? The second paragraph is loaded with what I call *powerful visual adjectives*. These PVAs produce clear, bright, high-impact *visual* images. They actually help your prospects demonstrate your products in their minds.

DON'T SAY:

Make lots of money!

DO SAY:

Rake in $2,750 cash weekly!

DON'T SAY:

Juicy Red Apples

DO SAY:

Mouth-watering, sugar-sweet, hand-picked apples!

DON'T SAY:

Drink cleaner water.

DO SAY:

Enjoy pure, crystal-clear, glacier-fresh water!

DON'T SAY:

Get a useful line of credit!

DO SAY:

Flash your credit card, and jewelry, electronics, home furnishings, and tropical vacations are yours!

DON'T SAY:

Earn good money selling gold at flea markets.

DO SAY:

Corner the gold market at high-traffic flea markets and watch the dollars come pouring in!

The Bath Soap Blow-Out

I have a nice head of hair. And it's a good thing. Because every so often I have a "discussion" with someone on this topic that leads me to rip much of it out. For example, I had a phone conversation with a friend whom I'm helping create a brochure. He and his wife sell home-made soap. Very nice soaps, actually. Beautiful colors and fragrances. Some look like nice big, juicy hunks of watermelon. Others resemble fresh orange slices, bright lemon wedges, and meaty chunks of coconut. Yum. (Do you see what PVAs—powerful visual adjectives—can do for your copy?) Here's the dialog, as I remember it...

Drew: Hey George...these fruity soaps are great. But why just blandly say, "Orange-Scented Bar Soap"? or "Coconut-Scented Bar Soap"? Why not compare them to the freshest, juiciest slices of Florida oranges? Why not talk about how washing your face with it is like splashing your skin with liquid sunshine? How the aroma reminds you of walking in the sunny, breezy orange fields of Florida? And your coconut soap—yum! Why just say, "Smells like real coconut"? Why not compare it to the freshly cut coconuts in the sun-soaked western Caribbean... reminiscent of the milky-white meaty centers and the sweet, luscious juice?

129

George: That seems a little over the top, don't you think? After all, we're not selling food, we're selling soap!

Drew: Ugh. [To myself.] Of course you're selling *soap*, George, but you want to create some romance...some imagery...something that people can latch onto. It's called *selling*.

George: All that doesn't seem necessary.

Drew: Necessary?! It's not *necessary* to sell soap, George! But if you *are* going to do it, why not do it well? Why not do it aggressively? Why not do more than your competition is doing? You're not the only one in this business, you know.

George: Uh huh.

Drew: These soaps are great! But you need to do more than your competition. You need to stand out!

George: Well, if what you're saying is so great, why doesn't anyone else do it?

Drew: Simple. Because most people don't do things the best possible way. They do what they *think* is best. And since most businesspeople don't know much about creating effective advertising, they don't do what could be most effective!

George: [Thinking. It sounds like a field of crickets.]

Drew: You're selling specialty soaps. Not Ivory, Zest, or Irish Spring. You're selling *expensive* soap that has two things going for it: (1) It *looks* beautiful, and (2) it *smells* delicious. Not playing up the two things that make your soap so appealing is a giant mistake! People don't buy your soap because they simply need to get clean. They can get clean with a cheap bar of Ivory.

George: Yes...but people will know how it smells *when they buy it*. Plus, everyone knows what oranges, coconuts, and lemons smell like. They smell like oranges, coconuts, and lemons.

Drew: [To self.] Dear God, help me.

George: ...so why take all that space to describe it to people who already know?

Drew: Because it helps persuade! Look at it this way: if someone sees your brochure, and that someone likes the smell of oranges, then she is going to be romanced by a description that's in keeping with what she likes. (Read that again.) It helps her imagine! It takes up more "space" in her brain by creating a mental movie of the product! Describe the juicy wedges, the sunny fields, the handpicking that goes on in the orchards, that sweet bursting of aroma when you peel one. And don't stop there! Create a *deep mental hook* with a phrase she won't be able to shake. Something such as: "The Orange-Juicy Way to Wash!" Don't call it "lather," call it "Sweet Orange-Cream Bubbles."

George: [Stifles laughter.] I hear what you're saying, Drew, but all those fancy descriptions...I can't get over the fact that we're just selling soap.

Drew: [Looking at watch.] Well, George, that's my advice. And I've been doing this for only 28 years. I'm sure you'll do whatever you feel is right for you. Gotta run!

[The sound of ripping brown hair.]

Remember: The more specific your words—described with PV's—the clearer the pictures. Even if your product or service is similar to your competitors', you can still stand out by using this technique.

EXAMPLE #1: Cleaning Service

DON'T SAY:

"Our expert cleaners will make your office sparkle like new."

DO SAY:

"We make your walls and floors hospital-bright, your restrooms sparkling and sanitized, your windows gleaming clean, and your carpets fluffy, fresh, and deodorized."

EXAMPLE #2: Italian Restaurant

DON'T SAY:

"People love our authentic Italian food because we prepare it like we do for our own family. Try it, it's delicious!"

DO SAY:

"We make our pasta fresh every morning. We bake our own bread, golden and crusty.

Our sauce is made from scratch—never from cans. Everything we serve is homemade, 100 percent natural, and delicious."

131

CA$HVERTISING Tip: The business that doesn't play the "PVA game" automatically loses. Because the advertisers that use this technique give the impression that they're more qualified, better equipped, more conscientious, and better able to meet their customers' needs. Why? Because they're the only ones telling the whole story, which automatically gives the impression that the others don't do these things. It's a devilishly potent psychological tool that sends the competition scrambling because they'll quickly realize the disadvantage you've thrust upon them.

Ad-Agency Secret #18:
Directing Mental Movies

Answer these questions honestly:

1. Would you rather eat a fruit tart, or a big slice of deep-dish bing cherry pie made from freshly picked, organic fruit, and a flaky, handmade, buttery crust, topped with a big scoop of double-churned vanilla-bean ice cream? Ooooh, look how all the sweet cherry juice flows out every time your fork sinks into that nice, thick slice. Yeah...put a little whipped cream on it, will ya? Wow...did you ever see so much fruit?!

2. Would you be more repulsed by having to kill a few bugs, or having to destroy an active nest of angry black widow spiders, including a quivering web of their just-hatched-hot eggs, guarded by their mindless, poison-fanged mother? Don't forget that just one female black widow can blow out four to nine egg sacs every summer, each containing up to 750 eggs incubating a fresh new load of up to 750 spiderlings in just 14 to 30 days. Worse still, each venomous arachnid lives—no, mates and breeds!—inside your home with your children and pets, for up to three full years!

   Try killing them yourself if you must, but think about this: If you miss killing just one egg-engorged female (or one of her hundreds of nearly microscopic crawling babies), you'll suffer a full-blown arachnid infestation in no time! I've been at war with black widows for the past five years, and there's nothing worse than feeling something crawling across your skin at night when you're in bed. Well,

132

actually, *one* thing *is* worse...discovering that the "queen mother" blew out a pile of fresh hot eggs under your pillow!

Do you see what I did? My careful word selection made plain old pie far more appealing. And—ugh—that "little" spider problem (that you otherwise would have handled yourself) now turns into a worthwhile $89 call to the exterminator. So what's happening here?

First, realize that all experience is made up of only these five factors—V-A-K-O-G:

1. Visual (sight).
2. Auditory (sound).
3. Kinesthetic (feeling or emotions).
4. Olfactory (smell).
5. Gustatory (taste).

These elements—our senses—are the ingredients of experience. Any time we experience anything in life, a blend of these elements is always present. We call these elements "IRs"—internal representations—because they represent our experience of the world around us internally, in our heads. In fact, memory is just a blend of these elements. Whenever you recall any experience, whether it's the pizza you ate yesterday, or the roller coaster you screamed on 28 years ago, you're accessing a blend of these five elements; a set pattern that "equals" your experience.

To boost the effect of your words—no matter what kind of advertising you're writing, be it ads, brochures, sales letters, flyers, e-mails, Websites, billboards, or radio or TV commercials—what you need to do is increase the strength of the representations in your prospects' brains. You need to ramp up the intensity of the five elements so that you create a *concentrated* internal experience with sufficient power to affect his or her behavior. This, my friend, is the secret recipe for getting people to take action.

Let's fact it: Your prospects are busy living their lives. They don't care about you or your product, but only how your product or service can make their lives better. In most cases, for most products and services (there are exceptions), you yourself mean absolutely nothing to them. (Gasp!)

"Drew! That's so cynical! How can you say something so horrible?" *Relax.* It's just a way of looking at the whole process. It goes back to the old maxim, "People don't buy your product for its features; they buy it for its benefits." So the way we get people to act, to buy, to ask for more information, is to take what's otherwise a dull, fuzzy image in their brains, and turn it into a sharp, super-focused, loud, colorful, tasty, fragrant, highly sensory experience.

Own a karate school? Don't just tell parents that you'll teach their kids to be more confident and get better grades. *Every* school says that! Also say that their kids will never become a punching bag for the schoolyard bully, with his dirty face, foul mouth, and clenched fists. (Feel the difference?)

"But Drew, no one writes copy like that! A karate school typically says, "We teach your child self-confidence and discipline, and give a free uniform when you enroll.' They don't say any of that 'dirty face, foul mouth' stuff!"

That's because (1) they don't think to write this way, and/or (2) they're afraid to write this way for fear of what people might think, or (3) they're duplicating everyone else's mediocre ads. It's a form of "business in-breeding," and the end result is weak, mutant advertising that means nothing to anybody.

Stop being afraid to use your own brain. Forge your *own* path and leave your *own* mark. You don't need permission from anybody to do things your way. You be the leader. You be the one people copy because what you're doing is so unique. Shake people up in your industry. Why be just another person in your industry who does nothing new, nothing worth noting, nothing that gets people talking and buying?

Okay, did you see what we did in that spider example? We simply enlarged, or heightened the IRs, the *internal representations* in our reader. We metaphorically grabbed our reader by the arms and shook him up. With our clear (visual) and nauseating (kinesthetic) description, We now occupy far more space in his brain. And by doing so we have effectively activated more brain cells by causing him to think more deeply (central route processing, remember?) about his (now repulsive) spider ordeal. And whenever you occupy more of people's brains, you're far more likely to persuade them. More likely to get them to act. We took fuzzy images (those with little color and detail) and sharpened them to crystal clarity.

This is why long copy consistently outsells short copy. It's why a salesperson who spends two hours with you will typically outsell a salesperson who spends five minutes. More time and more words lead to more persuasion.

What do you sell? How can you "beef up" your descriptions? How can you take your reader on a tour of your products or services?

As an example, I just bought an automatic pool cleaner. You hook it up to the dedicated suction line in your pool and throw it in. It vacuums up the bottom of your pool and keeps it clean. You can leave it in full-time if you want, and safely swim while it's running. It costs $250 and comes with a two-year warranty.

Okay, now assume you have a pool, but no pool cleaner. Are you ready to buy from my description? I doubt it. But why not? After all, I told you what it does, how to hook it up, what it costs, that it's effective, and that it comes with a two-year warranty! What the heck more do you need to know? Seems to me you have everything you need to make a buying decision. I even gave you my testimonial! The fact is, you did not buy because you were not sold. You're not buying because you have not amassed sufficient internal representations to spend money. You have facts, yes, but facts alone create few IRs. Facts alone do not prime the brain to buy.

So what do I need to say to motivate you to buy this product? I simply need to create visual IRs, auditory (sound) IRs, kinesthetic (feelings or emotion) IRs, olfactory (smell) IRs, and maybe even gustatory (taste) IRs—as many as practical—and tour you through the use of the product. My goal is to make my words so clear that you actually demonstrate the product in your mind before you buy it. For example:

Dear Scott,

Oh my God, this new pool cleaner I just installed is amazing! You HAVE to buy one for your own pool! It's by far the easiest pool cleaner I've ever used, and believe me, I did my research.

It's a long, ribbed plastic hose that attaches to your vacuum line or skimmer. It looks like a blue manta ray (about 2 feet long), and it skims gracefully across the bottom of the pool. It almost looks alive, so I named it "Squidly Diddly." :-)

Anyway, Squidly climbs the walls, and sucks all the leaves, sand, and other nasty stuff through its tiny mouth and conveniently deposits it into your filter basket for quick removal.

He even comes with a video that helps you put it together in less than 10 minutes. It's so easy my retriever Giuseppe could do it!

The company is well-known in the industry and has sold more than 1,250,000 of these cleaners worldwide. I did a ton of research before buying it, and all the reviews are favorable, far better than other pool cleaners in this price range. Price? It was only $250 and comes with a two-year warranty, and a $50 rebate!

I had one question and got someone on the phone fast...she was really friendly and helpful.

(Ha! While I was typing this, my wife came into the house and told me that the pool filter was LOADED with the junk that Squidly slurped out. This thing really works like crazy!)

[NOTE FROM DREW: The paragraph above is part of the sell copy. It's worded to "step out of" the context of an ad and convey a sense of "here and now," or real-time authenticity, as I discussed at the start of this chapter.]

Squidly makes a funny chuga-chuga-chuga sound when he's doing his job, but he's pretty darn quiet. He works so well we had to put a bucket near the filter so we had a more convenient place to dump all the junk he sucks out of our pool. (Remember how brown and muddy-looking our pool was last week? You should see the water now...it sparkles like a Caribbean lagoon, and I swear it even smells better too!)

Forget hand-vacuuming your pool! With my pal Squidly all I do is relax and sip piña coladas while he cleans the pool for me, day and night. He never misses a day, never complains, and never raises his prices. (Oh, by the way, I'm going to lay off Frank, the pool cleaner, next week. He's really a nice guy, but this automatic cleaner will save me $850 a year!)

The lesson is simple: Unless you create sufficient *internal representations* in your prospects' brains, you will insufficiently move them to mentally create their own IRs that ultimately cause them to pull out their wallets and buy what you're selling.

Of course, you won't always be able to use all five modes of internal representations. If you're a printer, for example, you're not going to tell people how wonderfully fruity your red and orange inks tastes (gustatory). But you could talk about how quality papers, glossy and smooth or rich with cottony texture (kinesthetic), can make their stationery so much more visually appealing, and how people will actually feel (kinesthetic) the quality when they hold their letters and brochures. This, in turn, translates into an unconscious association of quality with your company, and your products and services as well.

It's like jump-starting a car battery: Unless you apply enough juice, the car won't start. It's the same with the mental movies you install in your prospects' brains: Unless you create a "movie trailer" that's engaging enough to cause them to think more about what you're saying, they'll simply turn the page or click away to another site.

Ad-Agency Secret #19: Battling Human Inertia

I often begin my seminars in character: an old, stodgy salesman. I plant myself in a chair in front of my audience and drone on, in my most unenthusiastic voice, the most unmoving, uninspiring, unconvincing and un-*everything* sales pitch you could imagine. "No need to rush into the buying decision," I say. "Most likely dozens of other companies sell the same product at the same price, and offer you the same service. There's plenty of time; the product will be here when you need it."

Ugh! I then leap from my chair and shout, "If the old expression is true that advertising is nothing more than a salesperson in print, then THAT (pointing back to the chair I sprang from), I assert to you, is the typical salesperson that the average business has out there on the street representing them today!"

The point? No matter how slick a salesperson, no matter how beautiful an ad, if they don't cause people to take *action*, they're both a lousy investment. An ad that only *informs* and doesn't move people to buy is like a salesperson who can't close. Fire the salesperson. Trash the ad. They're wasting both your money and time.

> The simplest definition of advertising, and one that will probably meet the test of critical examination, is that advertising is selling in print.
>
> —Daniel Starch

Getting action requires two steps: (1) Make it easy to act, and then (2) ask for action.

Disclaimer: These ingredients do not *guarantee* people will act. If that were the case, then every ad you place that conformed to these two steps would be a smashing success. However, you *will* significantly raise the *chances* of your success. That would be okay, wouldn't it? So let's talk about Step 1: Make it easy to act.

As Joan Rivers says, "Can we talk?" We humans are lazy creatures. If we could push a button for almost everything that's now buttonless, we'd do it. Push-button shower? Push-button drive to work? Push-button push-button! In fact, there are few things left anymore that do not offer push-button convenience. We want to be satisfied *now*. We want results *yesterday*.

This means that people are hypersensitive to things that appear to be troublesome. We resist "getting involved."

For example, at the scene of a car accident a driver asks a bystander to be a witness. He replies, "Oh, I'd rather not get involved." The bystander is running a movie in his head filled with unpleasant scenes of all kinds of hassles, ordeals, and bothersome tasks requiring an unknown expenditure of energy. So he turns and walks away. And because people are hypersensitive to exerting themselves, and they do whatever they can to avoid effort, as advertisers it would be wise for us to make buying as easy as possible.

For example, did you ever get a direct-mail solicitation with an order form that's already filled in with your name and address? It requires you to do nothing more than add your credit card number or a check, and slip it into a postage-paid envelope that's also personalized with your return address. Today's digital printing makes this easy and cost-effective. There's also a toll-free phone number. Maybe they even let you pay C.O.D. because they know if they do most of the work *for* you, they're removing roadblocks that might prevent you from ordering. They're greasing the slide, so to speak, and looking for an unconscious "Gee, look how easy!" response.

Accept as many alternate forms of payment as possible: all the major credit cards, personal checks, money orders, and PayPal. You should offer several shipping options, from regular ground to overnight express (you could lose business if you don't ship fast enough). Gift-wrapping saves your customers time and effort on birthdays and holidays. Offer a strong guarantee to quell their fear of loss. Offer a payment plan—"Just $14.99 a month for three months"—to reduce the psychological pain of spending money. Offer Web ordering, especially when your competition doesn't. Tell your prospects exactly *how* to order, step by step. If you're a retailer, always provide your address, phone, and concise driving directions (not everyone uses a GPS) and your daily hours. Say, "It's Easy To Order!" And use variations of it that are suitable for your type of business: "It's Easy to Get a FREE Estimate!" or "It's Easy to Schedule Your Home Inspection!" or "It's Easy to Get Business Cards Printed for 50 percent Off!" or "It's Easy to Steam Clean Your Own Carpets & Save $199!" and an endless stream of variations. People want more ease in their lives. *Tell* them how easy it is to buy from you.

Ad-Agency Secret #20: Establish Your Unique Selling Proposition

If you've attended my seminars, you know that I'm adamant about using some type of gimmick or USP—unique selling proposition—to differentiate yourself in the market. You don't want to be like a 5-pound bag of sugar or salt in the grocery store, do you? Few people are fussy about what brand of sugar or salt they buy. To them, sugar is sugar. Salt is salt. In fact, ask a friend, "What's your favorite brand of salt?" He'll look at you like you're nuts.

The truth is, most people don't care much about these commodity products. They don't stand out. They blend in with other brands. The result? *They are not preferred.*

Fact: When people can't distinguish you from your competition, they have no reason to *prefer* you. And your goal in business is to have people *prefer* your product, to choose *you* over everyone else offering the same or a similar thing.

I grew up in northeast Philadelphia. About a mile from my home was (and still is) a little '50s-style diner called Nifty Fifty's at the busy corner of Grant Avenue and Blue Grass Road. This place does an incredible job of differentiating itself from its competitors—the lunch and

139

dinner lines busting through their doors onto the sidewalk prove it. It's located in a shopping center built about 30 years ago. In its exact location was a dance studio, a woman's fitness center, a Mexican food joint, a video rental store, and I don't recall *what* else. But it's the only business that has succeeded—and in a major way—and has now expanded to five locations. No wonder: The place just does everything right. In fact, check out the awards page on the Website at *www.niftyfiftys.com*—it's phenomenal. And this is the whole point: *the proprietors don't keep their greatness to themselves.*

> Don't try to be amusing. Spending money is a serious matter.
>
> —Claude Hopkins

On the contrary. They take every opportunity to make sure you know how wonderful they are, by making sure *you* know that they *never* use frozen beef, that their hamburger beef is ground fresh daily, that their French fries are fresh-cut and homemade, that they never use frozen onion rings. In fact, as soon as you walk through the front door, you can look through a big glass window into the kitchen and see the man wearing the paper hat dipping the big, juicy-sweet onion slices into their homemade batter and then into their wonderful, herb-seasoned breading. They tell you what kind of oil they fry in. They tell you why it's to *your* advantage to eat there rather than Burger Slop down the block. They don't just leave it up to you and hope you discover these things, like 99.9 percent of other businesses do. They're *proactive*. They toot their own horn. They *tell* you why they're great.

Think! What interesting story can you tell people about your product or service? How can you educate them?

CA$HVERTISING Tip: Be sure your product or service is one of excellent quality, or you may educate your potential buyer *away* from you!

* Don't be just a hardware store...be "The Hardware Superstore!"
* Don't be just an office cleaner...be "The Office Cleaning Technicians!"
* Don't be just a small pet shop...be "A World of Pets Under One Small Roof!"

* Don't be just a graphic designer who lives in Denver...be "Denver's #1 Graphic Design Persuader!"
* Don't be just an ice-cream shop...be "The Home of Monster Dip!"
* Don't be just a real estate sales office...be the "Experts of the RapidSell System!"

If you don't have a "RapidSell System," then get creative and put together a program that you can *call* the RapidSell System. Sometimes developing your USP requires that you *do* things differently, not just develop a hot tag line. Just *saying* you're an expert doesn't make you one. Your positioning should reflect what's true about you. And if you think up a great USP but it's not quite who you are, then *make* it who you are!

For example, if I wanted to call myself the Office Cleaning Technicians, but my staff looked like a bunch of unmotivated bums dressed in sloppy street clothes, my "Cleaning Technicians" positioning wouldn't go very far, would it? The word would spread that my people aren't technicians at all, but slovenly bums. So what would I do?

First, I'd hire people who look and act the part. (Image goes only so far. There comes a time when you have to perform and quality performance is the thing that gets you repeat business.) Next, I'd dress my people all in "hi-tech" blue or orange jumpsuits with my newly designed logo on their sleeves. I'd repaint my van and have a designer put my new image on each. I'd redesign my stationery and hire a designer to create a fresh new brochure incorporating the clean, modern look I'd want to portray. *Now* my "Technician" positioning has a chance to make it in the marketplace. Now it's backed up with something other than just an impressive tag line. What I *say* I am and how I'm *perceived* are now congruent. This is how you make your business fit your new positioning.

My CA$HVERTISING seminar prompted a woman to stop referring to herself as just another printer, and instead start powerfully promoting her services as "The Business Image Maker!" And to back up her claim, she submits articles to her local newspaper and business publications telling readers how to get the most for their printing dollar. She offers free reports such as, "How to Use 10 Little-Known Printing Secrets to Make Your Business Look More Professional," "How to Use the Power of Color to Make Your Business Materials Stand Out!"

and others. The reports are simply one to four pages and are a snap to produce.

She also holds free printing clinics at libraries for local businesses where she shows samples of good printing and bad, and tells her audience how to avoid making the same mistakes. She tells them how to get the most bang for the buck. She explains how to save thousands by knowing the latest digital printing technology and more. They love her, and in return they give her their business. Her image helps her by positioning her—and not her competition—as the go-to expert they can trust. This woman went from simply running a printing press to being a credible expert in her local area. And so can you.

Not only can you position your entire business, but you can also position your *offer*. For the following examples, I'm going to use ads from the direct-marketing industry. Late-night infomercials that claim to teach you how to make gobs of cash are more prolific than tech nerds at a PC convention. This is where great positioning is really needed for your ads to stand out.

For example, which of these two headlines attracts your attention most?

Work from Home and Turn Your E-Mail Into Big Profits!

19-Year Old College Kid Discovers Clever Way to Persuade People to Send You Money Via PayPal.

Which did you pick? If you have the marketing and advertising savvy I think you do, then you probably picked the one about the college guy, because it's what I call "specifically unique." It puts clear—not vague—pictures in your head. And when you do this, you have a stronger hold on your readers' attention. They're more engaged. They're wondering, "What *about* this 19-year old kid? How did *he* discover this idea?" They probably imagine what he must look like: his face, hair, clothing. Although there are thousands of "Make Money" ads, people have not heard this *positioning* before. It's fresh and different.

Tip: If you want your ad to stand out from the crowd, say something different.

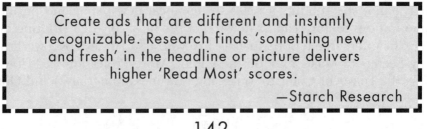

Create ads that are different and instantly recognizable. Research finds 'something new and fresh' in the headline or picture delivers higher 'Read Most' scores.

—Starch Research

Other examples:

Chinese Billionaire Reveals 14 Secrets That Helped Make Him So Rich.

With Just Four Months Left to Live, Millionaire Agrees to Reveal His Secrets of Wealth & Success.

Millionaire's Private Diary Found in Palm Springs— Reveals Little-Known Secrets of Success.

Get it? The point is to create a hook (or positioning) that's different from what thousands of other advertisers are saying. Be truthful, but find an intriguing way to say it! Stop all the "Get Rich Online" nonsense; people are tired of this vague, generic stuff. Ask yourself, "What's unique about my offer? Am I the only one offering this plan, product, or service? What's unique about me that I can exploit?"

Are you a farmer with a great cash-generating idea to sell to others in your industry? "Idaho Farmer Says, 'Growing $100 Bills Is as Easy as Growing Potatoes When You Follow My Plan!'"

Did you shave your head? "Big Bald Chris Teaches Wing Chun Kung Fu that Might One Day Save Your Life." Make sure you put a picture of yourself on everything and you'll become well known very quickly.

Are you a big or tall man or woman? *"6'5", 275-Pound Man Offers the BIGGEST Computer Discounts in the Nation!"* Have a photo of you taken from floor level to emphasize your size. Print it everywhere. Call yourself The Computer Giant! (In Pennsylvania, Big Marty's Carpets has been doing this effectively for years. Their ads and signs really stand out...big!)

Are you a great fisherman or woman involved in network marketing? "Fishing Expert Says, "Hooking PEOPLE is as easy as hooking flounder when you follow my secret plan to build up your down-line!"

Read the book *Positioning: The Battle for Your Mind*. It takes you step-by-step through the process of creating your image based on where you are now in the market, and where you want to be.

As I shout in my seminar, "Don't just be the *generic* version of what your business is! Let your competition blend in with all the others—not you! Give your image a twist, and stand up and stand out!"

Ad-Agency Secret #21:
Buy Your Own Island

Why pay for a full-page ad if you can dominate the page with one that costs less? Tell your ad rep you want a *Half-Page Island*: In contrast to a typical vertical or horizontal half-page, this special size is positioned so it visually takes up almost the entire page and makes it very difficult for the newspaper to put other ads near it.

The result? They often set only reading matter (news) next to your ad, which means less ad competition for you. The Half-Page Island is two columns wide and three-quarters of a page deep, yet it commands the *entire* page, which might—according to the principle of the Length-Implies-Strength heuristic discussed in Consumer Psychology Principle #17—cause readers to have greater feelings of your superiority. It's the old "The biggest ads in the *Yellow Pages* must be the better, more successful companies" effect.

Remember: You don't need giant ads for great response. Tiny little ads—like those repeated for years, unchanged, in magazines such as *Popular Science* and *Popular Mechanics*—have made many advertisers rich. Because of their space limitations, however, they're best for the ol' two-step sales process: (1) prospects inquire, and (2) you send the full info, which—we hope—causes them to buy. If you're looking to do more of a complete selling job, you'll need more real estate to tell your story. The Half-Page Island gives you this, while letting *your* story—not your competitors'—take the spotlight.

Ad-Agency Secret #22:
Authority Positioning

Are you an authority on your topic? The Cues of Life model tells us that authority figures have a great deal of credibility. Therefore, the claims they make are widely believed. Using the mental shortcut of peripheral processing, they rationalize that an authority knows what he's talking about. After all, he must have studied his topic for years (Length-Implies-Strength), people everywhere listen to him so it must be okay if I do too (Bandwagon Effect), he's impartial and relates only the facts, not opinions (Message Sideness, Evidence), so I can rely on what he says.

The fact is, you too can adopt such a position—market yourself as an authority in your field—and wear this same coat of influence. Let's start with the assumption that you already have an excellent grasp on your subject and can talk about it with fluency, because we want to discuss how to *position* yourself as an authority, not how to develop the study habits to acquire sufficient knowledge to make the claim.

Step 1: Begin to regard yourself as someone who has a mountain of valuable information to share with others. Simple, right? Unfortunately, low self-esteem keeps many people from taking even this first step. If you don't think your knowledge is valuable, you're doomed before you begin.

Step 2: Make what you know available to the public in as many forms as possible. How? First, go to a local commercial photographer and have a headshot taken of yourself wearing attire that's appropriate for your business. Then—and this is no time to be shy—begin printing it on *all* your sales materials. From brochures to contracts, get your face in front of the public. Put it in ads, e-mails, Web pages, sales letters, billboards! Then do a little self-publishing. Start an e-zine. Create several three- to 10-page reports on your subject in both hardcopy and PDF formats.

For example, let's say you're a printer. How about creating some simple reports entitled:

How to Get Beautiful Wedding Invitations Printed without Getting Ripped Off

How [YOUR CITY] Businesses Can Save Up to 27% on Beautiful 4-Color Printing

How to Make Your Resume 325% More Attention-Getting Than Your Competition

See what I mean? The report consists of information that you as a printer *already* know. In the resume example, your report can simply talk about things such as using special papers, typestyles, foils, and inks in order to make a super-professional impression and stand out in the crowd.

The reports would feature your headshot right on the cover, with your name in a caption under the photo, and your business name on the cover. For example, I'd do it this way:

INSIDE...

Printing Expert Reveals
How to Make Your Resume 325% More Effective
& Knock Out Your Competition!

A Special Report Prepared by:

Drew Eric Whitman
Business Printing Expert

Whitman Press, Inc.

821 Digital Road
Litho, CA 92261
(760) 555-5678

Inside, you begin with a few paragraphs about the importance of an attractive resume. Then follow that up with numbered ideas:

RESUME RESPONSE BOOSTER #1: Layout & Design

Resumes are like any other business communication. But in this case, the product you're selling is you! So your resume, cover letter, and envelope should be as attractive as those used by today's biggest corporations when they communicate with *their* prospective buyers. I've printed the resumes for some of the most talented people in their fields. And in every case, I've advised them to...

RESUME RESPONSE BOOSTER #2: Paper Selection

And so on.

What do you do with these reports? You advertise them in your ads. You offer them free to anyone who comes into your shop. Not only do they promote you as an authority, but they also make people comfortable with you. And while 99 percent of your competition is doing absolutely nothing to raise their image to the public, you are positioning yourself as an authority. Remember to include a coupon with the report. If you did a good job, by the time they finish it, they should be primed to do business with you because you're now regarded as someone who knows what they're talking about on the topic of resume printing!

How else can you promote yourself as an authority? Create editorial-style ads for your local newspaper that look like question-and-answer columns. *You* make up the questions and *you* make up the answers. Include about three questions with short answers in each column, and make sure your headshot appears at the top with your name as the caption. In fact, some papers will accept your "column" for free if it offers useful information to its readers. In any event, make sure to include your business name, address, and phone number at the bottom of the ad in this sneaky way: "Have questions about how to use printing most effectively? Send them to: [your address here]."

Give seminars, hold workshops, create educational products, write a book, do radio and TV interviews, blog your expertise! There's no limit to the number of ways you can help others, which, in turn, can also do wonders for your business.

Ad-Agency Secret #23:
A Sales Letter in Survey's Clothing

I've done this for virtually every major client with whom I've worked, and it never fails to produce great returns. What you do is mail a survey to your customers asking them five or six questions about whatever it is you'd like information about: How they feel about your product or service, what they think about your prices, if they'll likely buy from you in the next month or two. In other words, ask them questions that will give you valuable insight into their thought processes.

Then, at the bottom of the survey, make them an appealing offer they can't refuse. Maybe it's a coupon for 50 percent off their next purchase, or a certificate for a free consultation, or a voucher good for a special gift the next time they buy—whatever you think would be appealing. Next, you write a short letter saying something similar to this:

Dear Eileen:

May I ask you a favor?

I'd like to know your honest opinion of our Deluxe Auto Detailing Service we performed for you recently.

Would you kindly check off your answers to the questions below, and then mail this survey back to me in the postage-paid envelope enclosed? Thanks for being such a great customer.

Sincerely,

[SIGNATURE]

Drew Eric Whitman, owner, Shimmy Shine Shop

Circle One (1) Number for Each of the Questions Below...

1) On a scale from 1 to 10 (10 being the best), how happy are you with our Deluxe Detailing?

1 2 3 4 5 6 7 8 9 10

Not happy   Very happy

2) On a scale from 1 to 10 (10 being the best), what do you think about our service?

1 2 3 4 5 6 7 8 9 10

Poor   Excellent

And so on and so forth. Now, the key part is at the end of the survey, and here's how it looks.

Thanks, Eileen! To show my appreciation for your completing this important survey, I'm sending you this 16-ounce bottle of *Liquid Mirror Spray* for **50% OFF** to protect your car's just-detailed finish. Simply spray on and wipe off. It's regularly $10, but I'll send it to you—postage paid—for just $5 when you return this completed survey by [DATE]. This important product helps keep your car shining and seals out dirt for up to 50% longer when you apply it within 30 days of your detailing, so don't wait! Protect your investment. Simply **CHECK THE "YES" BLOCK BELOW** and return this survey with your payment. A regular $10 value, it's my way of saying "Thank You" for participating in my survey.

HALF-PRICE SPECIAL AVAILABLE ONLY TO SURVEY RESPONDENTS!

[ ] YES, DREW! I have completed your survey as you asked. Please send me a $10 can of Liquid Mirror Spray for just 5 bucks. That's a 50% discount available only for people who respond to this special survey. [ ] Cash [ ] Check [ ] Money order [ ] Credit Card: [ ] VISA [ ] Mastercard Card#_____ Exp._____

Do you see the power of this? What it does is capitalize on the fact that (1) people love giving their opinion on things, and (2) because they're already returning their survey, it's so easy for them to slip their payment into the postage-paid return envelope.

The key is to offer something you would have offered anyway, but make it available only to those people who reply to your survey. The fact that you say the low price is "your way of saying thank-you" is a great qualifier for the low price, and gives an air of exclusivity to the offer.

The survey format is a snap. It's simply a personal letter on an 8 1/2 × 11-inch sheet of your business stationery. Mail-merge it so your letters look personal, and not mass produced, for best response.

You can use this survey technique for most any product or service. On top of additional sales, you'll also get valuable feedback. In fact, the feedback could be worth more than the profit you earn from the additional sales! One great question to ask to get people to express themselves freely is, "If *you* were the owner of my business, what would *you* do differently?" You'll be amazed at some of the great answers you'll get. The feedback you receive could completely alter the way you run your business. See Ad Agency Secret #28: Survey Power for more information about turning your customers' thoughts into profits.

Ad-Agency Secret #24: Power Your Ads With Pictures

Everyone knows the expression, "A picture is worth a thousand words," but most don't know that this idiom is backed by scientific research.

In 1991, Roper Starch Worldwide conducted a study of 2,000 consumers in 10 U.S. markets who responded to 650 newspaper ads in a large variety of retail and national categories. The results scientifically proved how the inclusion of pictures, whether photos or illustrations, directly impact advertising response—no matter what type of product or service is being promoted. Here are the results of that study.

* Ads consisting of 50 percent visuals (photos, illustrations, graphics elements) were noted (seen and recalled) 30 percent more often than ads with no visuals.

* Ads consisting of 75 percent visuals are noted 50 percent more often than ads with few or no visuals.

* In the "Read Most" category, these same ads also scored 60 percent higher.

149

* Four to nine visuals boost "Noted" scores by 30 percent over ads with fewer or no visuals.

* Ads with 10 or more visuals are 55 percent more likely to be Noted than ads with fewer or no visuals.

* "Read Most" scores jump by 70 percent for ads with 10 or more visuals.

* Showing the product attracts readers 13 percent more often than showing no product.

* Photos are the most compelling type of graphics and attract the greatest readership.

The Seven Best Types of Photos

Multiple studies show that the following types of photos attract the most attention. In a classic survey performed for the Kimberly-Clark Corporation by the Gallup Research Bureau, called "Let 4,979,855 readers tell you what they read on Sunday," 29,000 readers of 20 different Sunday newspapers in 16 cities were questioned. Gallup found that readers preferred the following pictures, listed in order of preference:

1. Children and babies.
2. Mothers and babies.
3. Groups of adults.
4. Animals.
5. Sports scenes.
6. Celebrities.
7. Food.

Parade magazine once reported that the following pictures get the greatest attention:

1. Babies.
2. Mothers and babies.
3. Animals.
4. Personalities.
5. Food pictures.

Why are these pictures so appealing to us? Because they tap into our Life-Force 8 desires. We want love, to protect and care for our family, social acceptance, the drive to win, status, and food and drink. In Douglas Adams's *The Hitchhiker's Guide to the Galaxy*, the meaning of life is "42." In reality, the answer to most any "why" question you can ask about human beings is "8"—the Life-Force 8. Try it and see.

Pictures are only effective in influencing brand choice if there is a clear connection with the brand and message.
—Giep Franzen, *Advertising Effectiveness*, 1994

The Power of Demonstration, Action, and Pseudo-Movement

Placing a photo of your product in your ad attracts readers 13 percent more often than not showing it. Product-in-use shots add an additional 13 percent boost over product-only shots. Why? In-use photos add action, drama, interest, and demonstrate your product or service and engage readers' imaginations. Ads with photos or illustrations of people increase "noted" scores by nearly 25 percent over ads without any people or visuals.

In my CA$HVERTISING seminar I show examples of two ads for pepper spray for two competing companies. Company A's headline reads, "MUGGER STOPPER!" and features a close-up of a woman's hand holding the product as if she were showing you the label. Yawn. I can't think of another product that offers so much dramatic possibility, yet this company opted to show their product doing...er, nothing at all.

Company B, on the other hand, was smart. Their headline, "Stop Muggers at the Push of a Button!" showed an illustration of a woman spraying a group of sleazy-looking attackers who surround her in a semi-circle. Each of the thugs is shown in various stages of distress: on their knees, flat on the ground, coughing, grabbing their faces, screaming, and running away.

Now tell me, dear reader, if you saw only the headlines and the pictures, which of these two products would *you* prefer to carry if you were in the market for pepper spray? The answer is obvious. Company B gave you a demonstration—so to speak—of how its product works. And even though it's an illustration—black-and-white at that—(a photo would have been better), it still conveys a sense of the pepper spray's effectiveness, whereas Company A's crappy ad conveys nothing more than a sense of advertising ignorance.

151

> Always provide context for your photos. Instead of showing a refrigerator against a generic studio background, show it in a beautifully equipped working kitchen.
>
> —Starch Research

Ad-Agency Secret #25: Grab 'Em With Grabbers

What are *grabbers*? They're little items you attach to the top of the first page of your sales letter that grab people's eyes and make it nearly impossible for them not to read further, such as a penny, nickel, dime, quarter, or dollar bill.

If I sent you a letter with a $1 bill stapled to the top, wouldn't you be interested? It's just a dollar, but that letter would probably interest you more than anything else that arrived in the mail that day. Here's an example of how you can begin your copy using this technique. Let's say, for example, that I sell carpet and I got my hands on a list of people who just moved into the neighborhood.

Dear Scott,

As you can see, I have attached a crisp one-dollar bill to the top of this letter.

Why? To make a point.

I'm going to show you—right here in this letter—how to save 100 of these bills (yes, $100.00) when you buy carpet for your new home.

Or let's say I own a day spa and I mail to a list women within 5 miles of my business.

Dear Louise,

As you can see, I have attached a crisp one-dollar bill to the top of this letter.

Why? To make a point.

I'm going to show you—right here in this letter—how to save 20 of these bills (yes, $20.00) on your very first visit to Caribbean Blue.

Or let's say I'm a network marketer selling tropical mangosteen juice, and I mail the following to a list of opportunity seekers.

Dear Eric,

As you can see, I have attached a crisp one-dollar bill to the top of this letter.

Why? To make a point.

I'm going to show you—right here in this letter—how to make up to 10,000 of these bills (yes, $10,000.00) in less than three months, with the hottest new moneymaking program to hit the network marketing industry in decades!

Get it? It's a proven effective way to stir up your readers' curiosity—and maybe even make them feel a little obligated to at least read your letter. But there are many more grabbers than the lowly dollar. All kinds of things make interesting and effective eye-catchers.

For example, let's say I'm a crafty wedding photographer and I'm able to get a hold of a mailing list of women about to get married.

Dear Louise,

As you can see, I have attached a HORRIBLE wedding photo to the top of this letter.

Why have I done this? To keep YOU from making the same tragic mistake this poor couple did.

You see, Esther and Sam (the bride and groom) had no idea what to look for when they chose their wedding photographer.

The result? A crying shame! The lighting was crummy. The people look stiff. The angles are amateurish. The color is inconsistent. And even their skin-tone is blotchy. Their one big day and all they have to show for it is a bunch of mediocre photos.

Do YOU know how to avoid the mistake Esther and Sam made? I'll tell you how, right here in this letter.

You'd continue your letter with some helpful tips and then describe the advantage of your services. Include a sheet of testimonials (featuring your best photos, of course), and extend your money-saving offer. A good-looking "savings certificate" would add a nice touch.

* Do you sell Laguna Beach, California, real estate? Attach a little baggy of sand!

* Are you a collection agency? Attach an "NSF" check!

* A candy shop? Attach a wrapper from a bar of your finest chocolate and enclose a coupon good for a free sample of what was once inside that wrapper! (What a nasty trick!)

* A printer? Attach a poorly printed brochure.

The possibilities are endless! Just be sure that your grabber won't rip the envelope, or postal workers will see a slew of some very bizarre objects floating around in the mail stream! If you choose to use a bubble wrap–lined envelope, your options are even greater.

The technique works. It worked for Robert Collier way back in 1937, and it will work for you today. Skeptical? Test it! Do an A-B Split: A) Mail 500 sales letters *with* the grabber, and B) mail another 500 letters *without* the grabber. Compare the results, and I'll welcome you as the newest member of the Great Grabber Fan Club!

Ad-Agency Secret #26:
Long Copy vs. Short

Ah yes, the old *long copy vs. short* debate. I thought the argument was buried decades ago. Not just rotting dead, but bone-dry *dust* dead. The fact is, real-world (not academic) testing for nearly a century shows there's nothing left to debate. But some less informed people disagree.

> Direct response advertisers *know* that short copy doesn't sell. In split run tests, long copy invariably outsells short copy.
>
> —David Ogilvy

In fact, the one comment that immediately tells me someone knows very little about advertising goes this way: "Oh, you better keep the copy short! No one reads long copy. People are busier than ever these days. Keep it nice and short."

Although their warnings to keep it short might *sound* logical, it's utter nonsense! Direct response copy great Gary Halbert, an early mentor of mine, once wrote, "Copy can never be too long, only too boring!" How true.

154

Hundreds of studies and *thousands* of experiments have been done. And all the giants of advertising, John Caples, Claude Hopkins, David Ogilvy, John E. Kennedy, Eugene Schwartz, Maxwell Sackheim, Walter Weir, and all the other Copywriter Hall of Famers agree: Well-written *long* copy outsells short copy. No qualifications. No disclaimers. It simply *does*.

> The most common expression you hear about advertising is that people will not read much. Yet a vast amount of the best-paying advertising shows that people do read much.
>
> —Claude Hopkins

The fact is, if someone is a true prospect for your product, you wouldn't believe how much well-written sales copy he or she will read. Don't ramble with your copy, of course. Don't write simply to fill up space or to impress people with your vocabulary. But do write enough to inform, build desire, convince, and motivate people to take action. The old expression, "the more you tell, the more you sell" is true...*if* you tell it right.

Think about it: Would you be more likely to buy if you spent two hours with a good salesperson, or just 10 minutes? Two hours of course. Why, you'd hear every sales pitch in his repertoire, he'd hit you with every benefit he could conjure, he'd uncover—and then *push*—every one of your hot buttons, over and over again.

> The only reason for using short copy is when there isn't much to say.
>
> —Maxwell Sackheim

So why would people think their sales materials are so different than this salesperson? Of course, your ads, brochures, and sales letters can't judge feedback. They can't see what's turning the prospect on or off. That's why they have to cover all the bases. Restate each benefit from several different angles, and from several different perspectives.

Did you ever notice how many car commercials, for example, not only appeal to what *you're* going to think about your new car, but also what *others* think about it? Heads turn as the car whizzes by (Life-Force 8: social approval; keeping up with the Joneses). And practicality: it's so darned safe. Crash tests prove it. (Life-Force 8: survival; freedom from pain and danger; protection of loved ones). Notice how they appeal to not only your emotions, but also to logic and reason? This way they speak to both the peripheral *and* central-route thinkers.

But that's not all! The low price and high gas mileage ratings mean you're buying smart. You're responsible. (Life-Force 8: social approval.) And you can save money for the more important things in life, such as your kid's education, or a nice vacation with your spouse.

See what's happening? The more ways you justify the purchase of your product, the more likely you'll influence people to buy. So you take them by the hand and tell the whole story. You pile on the benefits (Length-Implies-Strength), show pictures to help them see it, slather on the testimonials (social proof), and back it up with a warranty (to quell fear). By the time you're done, you have quite a convincing (and often lengthy) sales piece. Keep it interesting and relevant. The more sell they're exposed to, the stronger the influence.

> A salesman does not say, "How do you do?" speak a few words about his product, then ask you to sign the order. No, he uses enough words to get your emotions and reasoning power flowing toward a sale.
>
> —Victor Schwab

Here's why I think most people don't get it: They think that people must read *all* the copy in order to buy. Nonsense! If I'm reading a long-copy ad or sales letter, for example, and I'm ready to buy after reading just the *headline*, I'll pick up the phone and place my order right then and there. I'm not going to say, "Shoot! I really wanted this thing, but there's more copy to read. Oh hell...now I can't order." *That's ridiculous!* Some people need long copy to be convinced; others can decide with less information. Long copy satisfies *both* parties. Ms. Long gets all her details. Mr. Short can stop reading whenever he wants to and place his order. On the other hand, if I used *only* short copy, I don't give Ms. Long what she needs, and she goes away unconvinced. How silly to create sales materials for only one type of buyer.

"But Drew, what about Web copy? That's totally different, right?" Wrong. Studies show that long copy outperforms short copy...yes, even online.

User Interface Engineering is a research, training, and consulting firm specializing in Website and product usability. Here's what they report.

1. "Our research shows that fewer, longer pages may be the best approach for users. In the trade-off between hiding content below the fold or spreading it across several pages, users have greater success when the content is on a single page."

2. "Increasing the levels of information, similar to adding sections to an outline, also seemed to help users."

3. "Users may tell us they hate scrolling, but their actions show something else. Most users readily scrolled through pages, usually without comment."

MarketingExperiments.com conducted several tests to see what impact copy length has on a Website's conversion rate.

Results: Long copy outperformed short copy in all three of their tests.

Despite internal debating about whether or not to try a long-copy approach, Online-Learning.com *quadrupled* the length of the copy on their homepage. Doug Talbott reported, "The number of people who left our site after viewing only the homepage has dropped by about 5 percent...we've also noticed that our enrollments have increased by about 20 percent."

If advertisers worried more about the *quality* of their sales materials, they wouldn't have time to worry about this ridiculous chicken-and-egg riddle. They'd be too busy ringing up sales.

> After you have found your most efficient-size ad, you should jam your space full of copy, no matter whether it is a one-inch ad or a full-page ad.
>
> —John Caples

Anyone debating me on this point is ridiculous. Anyone debating John Caples and the other advertising greats I've quoted in this section is an advertising knucklehead.

Ad-Agency Secret #27: Offer Testing

Just as you should test different headlines, it's vitally important to test different *offers*. Just because people don't respond to your ad, that does not mean they don't want what you're selling. Your ad may not have communicated effectively, or simply wasn't sufficiently appealing.

For example, let's say you're Dr. McCracken, chiropractor, and your current ad announces your grand opening. The ad seems great, but no one calls. So you rewrite your ad and you offer a free spinal evaluation. Or you offer 50 percent off their first visit. What you have done is change your offer. In fact, your Grand Opening wasn't offering anybody anything at all, was it? You were just telling people to be happy because you're in business. No good. You need to develop different offers and find out which works best.

How else could you frame your offer? How about instead of 50 percent off the first visit, you say, "2 Visits for the Price of 1!" It's the same thing as 50 percent off, isn't it? But testing has shown that "Buy One Get One FREE" is more effective than saying 50 percent off. *Free* is a powerful word.

What else could you say? How about "April Special: FREE Spinal Exams for Runners," then try, "May Special: FREE Spinal Exams for Body Builders," and so on. Why not try, "FREE Massage with Every Visit!" What could such an appealing offer do for your customer base? I don't care if you hire a massage school *student* to do the work, you'd be offering more than Dr. Vertebrae down the road, and giving people what they're looking for: *more!* Giving a free massage lets you make a *very* appealing offer in your ad, and can help you divert attention away from your competition that offers nothing extra.

Constantly ask yourself, "How can I give my customers more, knowing that they'll reward me with more business?" Isn't this what *you* want when you shop? Don't *you* want more for your money? Of course. What other offers can you make? How about a "Family Special?" Or a "Husband and Wife" deal? These are all different offers, different ways to position the deal. Keep testing different offers until you find one that delivers results that knock your socks off.

How about a special rate for seniors? How about every fifth visit is free? If you're a chiropractor who adjusts children's spines, how about, "Free Sammy the Smiling Skeleton With Every Child's Visit!" and put a picture of it in your ad. Sure, it's creepy, but who knows? It might bomb...or it might take your practice in a whole new profitable direction! That's precisely why you test. How about a free back support pad with every first visit? Or an authoritative-sounding report, "14 Things You're Doing Right Now That Are Torturing Your Back and Spine."

If your ads aren't working, don't throw in the towel and say "Nobody wants what I'm selling! Woe is me!" First try changing your headline, because this will make or break your ad in the first few seconds. Then check your price, because you could simply be out of line with the market. Then try a different offer.

Remember: What you're trying to do is find out what appeals to the marketplace. You can't tell the marketplace what to buy from you. *They* will tell you what *they* want. If your ad doesn't work, they are telling you. If your phone doesn't ring, they are telling you. If no one redeems your coupons, they are telling you. It's up to you to find out what they want and then give it to them. And that's the subject of...

Ad-Agency Secret #28: Survey Power

What's the best way to find out what people want? Ask them. That's exactly what salespeople started doing back in the 1930s. They approached cab drivers, homemakers, businessmen, construction workers, retailers—whoever fit the description of the target market they were after—and fired the questions at them: "What do you like? What do you dislike? What do you want? What would you prefer? How could it be better?"

The responses gave manufacturers invaluable feedback for new and improved products. It also gave their ad agencies ammunition to create campaigns that zeroed in on consumers' desires with the accuracy of a cruise missile, versus the fall-where-they-will gravity bomb campaigns they used before taking surveys.

It's no different today. And despite how it's portrayed on TV and in movies, working in an agency is not what most people think it is. You don't just sit around and dream up clever slogans. The process of developing a successful advertising campaign and accompanying materials does not begin with creative flashes. It begins with *research*.

For example, if you have the greatest bottled water in the world and you're trying to peddle it door-to-door in a city where the majority of residents have their own backyard wells, you're out of luck. You didn't do your research.

Instead of spending thousands of dollars running ads trying to guess what your customers or prospects want, why not simply ask them, and then create advertising around their responses! A clever shortcut, no?

So do a survey! Ask people what they think about your product or service. For example, if you run a pizzeria, ask people what things are most important to them when going out for pizza. What do they like? What do they hate? What's the most they'd pay for an 18-inch pie with the works? Would they come in more often if you offered two free drinks with every large pizza? What's their biggest complaint? How often do they go out for—or pick up—pizza?

To whom do you send this survey? How about everybody within a 5-mile radius of your pizzeria? Or maybe just your own customers. Offer a free slice as a thank-you for providing their feedback. Yep...*bribe* them to take your survey. And don't you dare gripe about this! The amount you spend on free slices is *insignificant* compared to the value of the information you'll receive. Limit the response time to keep it under control.

A good format for a survey is a double postcard. This is simply a postcard that's split with a perforation. One of the postcards has the address of the recipient on it. The opposite side explains the free goodies they get for completing and returning the survey card, which is the other side of the perforation. On the opposite side of the survey card is *your* return address. After completing the survey, your recipient simply tears on the perforation, separating both cards, and drops the survey card in the mail. For greater response, use a Business Reply Mail permit indicia on the reply card so people aren't put off by having to stamp it. Hey, you're getting valuable information, so make it as easy as possible for people to complete your survey!

Another simple format is a one-page letter-size survey. You'd mail your one-page letter explaining your great offer and enclose the one-page survey along with a postage-paid reply envelope addressed to your company. They'll read your letter, complete the survey, slip it into your self-addressed, stamped envelope, and pop it in the mail. Try to keep it short, and you may be able to get both your letter *and* survey on the front of one 8 1/2 × 11-inch page, on both sides if necessary. This will save paper and make the whole process less complicated to your recipient because there will be fewer papers to handle. The advantage of this format is that it's much easier to print yourself, and the letter and envelope format look more like a personal communication, which is likely to get greater attention. (Be sure to read Ad Agency Secret #14: The "Granny Rule" of Direct Mail for design tips for getting people to open your survey letter.)

Remember: The secret of good survey response is *ease*! Make it super easy to reply. Give all multiple-choice answers if possible, and use *semantic differential* scales. For example:

On a scale from 1 to 10, how likely are you to go out for pizza rather than make it yourself at home?

1 2 3 4 5 6 7 8 9 10

Not Likely to Go Out   Very Likely to Go Out

On a scale from 1 to 10, how much better is Franko's pizza compared to store-bought *frozen* pizzas?

1 2 3 4 5 6 7 8 9 10

Franko's Is Worse   Franko's Is Better

On a scale from 1 to 10, how likely are you to return to Franko's Pizza within the next two weeks?

1 2 3 4 5 6 7 8 9 10

Not Likely   Very Likely

Wouldn't it be a shame if, after spending thousands on a new promotion, hundreds on ads, and hundreds on your new brochure, you find out that what you're pushing isn't what your customers and prospects want? Ugh. You need to do your research *first*. And doing a survey is the easiest and most inexpensive way to do it.

Imagine the advantages you'll have over your competition, knowing exactly how your prospects feel, what they want, when they plan on returning, and even how much they'd pay! Now imagine how foolish you'll feel after tallying up all the responses and thinking about all those ridiculous promotions you ran offering the complete opposite of what they *really* wanted. I'm confident that few—if any—of your competitors have ever done it. Ad agencies respect the power of the survey and the incredible insight it provides. Try it once, and I guarantee you'll make it part of your standard practice.

Ad-Agency Secret #29: Editorial Energizers

You don't need to be related to Walter Cronkite to benefit from making your ads look like news stories. It's a tested and proven effective way to lift your response, and it's so easy to do. This incredibly simple idea is hailed by many of the best-known advertising professionals of all time.

David Ogilvy said editorial ads get 50 percent better readership. John Caples said 80 percent. Direct response specialist Richard Benson quotes 500 to 600 percent. Eugene Schwartz, one of the greatest direct response copywriters of all time, dedicates an entire section to this technique in his book *Breakthrough Advertising*. Schwartz calls the technique *camouflage* because the goal is to make your ad blend in with the publication's news stories. Here's how it works.

Let's say you're a professional hypnotist who specializes in helping people quit smoking. Instead of creating an ad that looks the same as every other ad in your local paper, you write your ad in news-article style. You have it set in the same typeface, the same column width, and the same leading (pronounced "ledding," and meaning the space between each of your lines) as that publication's news articles are set. Do the same for your headline too. Your "news ad" could start out something similar to this:

Local Hypnotist Announces New Way to Quit Smoking in 48 Hours

If you're an Orlando resident who wants to kick the habit, but you can't seem to muster the willpower, then this article brings you good news. Master Hypnotist and Orlando resident Burgess J. Halshire has discovered a new way to....

It's as simple as that. You just continue in that same manner, giving the same benefits as you would in a regular ad, but you couch them in the "news reporter voice."

A great technique is to work in a few quotes, such as, "I thought I'd never quit," said Scott Lawrence, one of Halshire's successful patients. "I tried absolutely everything, including locking myself in a mop closet for a week. It didn't work, and now I prefer smoking in mop closets."

After you've told your story, you push for action. "For more information about Halshire's powerful new 48-Hour Stop Smoking Technique, simply call his office at (407) 345-6789. Or visit him online at HalshireHypnosis.com"

CA$HVERTISING Tip: In editorial ads, never sound *too* enthusiastic about what you're selling. News reporting is supposed to be objective, so if you get too carried away, too "hypey," you'll blow the whole effect. It's a good idea to first read a few news stories from the publication before you sit down to write your ad. This will give you a feel for the tone you need to duplicate. For increased response, offer a free report to anyone who calls or visits your Website: "For a free copy of Dr. Halshire's report, 'How Hypnosis Can Help You Quit Smoking in 48 Hours,' simply call his office at (407) 345-6789. Or visit him online at HalshireHypnosis.com."

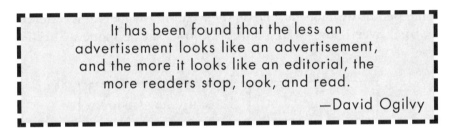

> It has been found that the less an advertisement looks like an advertisement, and the more it looks like an editorial, the more readers stop, look, and read.
>
> —David Ogilvy

Ad-Agency Secret #30:
The Coupon Persuader

Can a simple broken, coupon-style line around your ad help motivate people to buy? Yes indeed. Even if your ad is not an actual "money-off" coupon, this technique often lifts response because people are conditioned to read and act on coupons thanks to the financial rewards they suggest.

Who discovered this little moneymaker? All hail Mr. Asa Griggs Candler, the Philadelphia pharmacist who bought the Coca-Cola company from the soft drink's inventor, Dr. John Pemberton. Candler was considered a pioneer in coupon promotions. In 1894, Candler offered a refreshing glass of Coca-Cola free to anyone who redeemed one of his little hand-written tickets. This was so successful, he next offered two gallons of Coca-Cola syrup "to any retailer or soda fountain man" who would dispense 128 free servings (one gallon's worth) of the beverage to customers who presented one of his coupon cards. Candler's aggressive promotions drove Coca-Cola into every state and territory in the United States by 1895.

Don't ignore coupons, no matter what kind of business you're in. Little coupons bring big returns! Check these stats from the Coupon Council:

* 86 percent of the population of the United States uses coupons.
* Shoppers saved approximately $2.7 billion last year by using coupons.
* The typical coupon was worth $1.28 savings in 2007.
* Coupon users report an average of 11.5 percent savings on their grocery bill with coupons.
* Manufacturers offered more than $350 billion in coupon savings in 2007.

"Yeah, that sounds great, Drew, but only older people clip coupons; retired people with lots of time on their hands. My market is different." Not true! Everybody—young and old—loves saving money. Check out these stats.

Age	Percent Using Coupons
18–24	71
25–34	87
35–44	89
45–54	85
55–64	90
65+	91

"But Drew, only low-income people clip coupons!" Wrong again! In fact, the greatest percentage of coupon users earn up to $100,000 a year!

Income	Percent Using Coupons
Under $25,000	86
$25–$50,000	85
$50–$75,000	88
$75–$100,000	88
$100,000+	81

[Coupon stats courtesy of CMS, Inc., PMA Coupon Council]

The bottom line? People are coupon crazy! In fact, many will clip a coupon that saves them 50 cents and drive five miles out of their way just to redeem the damned thing. At today's standard car-mileage reimbursement of 56.5 cents, you don't need to be Einstein to see that this person is $2.32 in the hole.

But that's not all. Advertise *"Double Coupons!"* and some people drool with anticipation until the next Sunday's newspaper smacks on their doorstep. Well, you too can harness the psychological power of coupons. Simply surround your ad, order form, flyer, or reply coupon with a bold, broken, block-type border. I just wrote copy for a free bonus gift that my client will feature on his Website. I instructed the designer to set the copy within a coupon border of 3-point thickness with a very light yellow tint behind the text. What an eye-catcher!

When you use this idea, you're taking advantage of what's called an *anchor* in neuro-linguistic programming (NLP). An anchor is a conditioned response that's set off by the introduction of a particular stimulus. Russian scientist Ivan Pavlov rang the bell and fed the dog, rang the bell and fed the dog, rang the bell and fed the dog. Soon, after all these repetitions, he was able to make the dog drool by simply ringing the bell. The bell was the anchor. A link between the bell and the food was made in the dog's brain, and a "conditioned reflex"—copious drooling—resulted. To the dog, the bell actually *meant* food. Pavlov termed the response **signalization**, which later came to be known as classical conditioning.

CA$HVERTISING Tip: A coupon doesn't have to be a certain size to be effective. It can be anything from a tiny one-inch column ad (look in *Popular Science* for examples of some powerful little one-inch "coupon" ads) to a giant brochure. I like to use bold coupon borders where each "dot" that makes up the border is actually a little rectangle.

So, can you now see how a coupon acts as an anchor? In the human mind, a coupon means savings, it means a good buy, it means a smart shopper. And while it's not likely that you'll get anyone to drool over *your* coupon (if you do, please let me know; that's one technique I'm still trying to develop), you *can* take advantage of the positive feelings—either conscious or unconscious—that coupons stimulate; feelings that often lead to sales.

Ad-Agency Secret #31:
7 Online Response Boosters

1. Best Frequency for E-Mailing

How often should you e-mail for the best response? Forrester Research and NFO World Group both reported the identical conclusion that 31 to 35 percent of e-mail recipients prefer one mailing per week; 18 percent said two to three days per week; 13 percent said once a month; 12 percent said daily; 10 percent responded two to three times per month; 6 percent said less than once a month; and the NFO study reported that 8 percent replied "Never."

2. Click-Through Rates— Studies Tell What to Expect

Gas prices go up, e-mail response goes down. There's no correlation, but it's a reality we all must face. Studies show that click-through rates for e-mail marketing are declining. Currently you can expect anything from less than 1 percent in response to poorly crafted offers e-mailed to rented lists, to more than 20 percent for offers containing highly appealing incentives sent to your own customer list.

Remember: Click-throughs do not mean orders, but to make the sale your audience must, of course, first read your message.

3. The HTML vs. Text Conundrum

According to *Opt-In News*, more than 68 percent of all e-mail marketing is in HTML (hypertext markup language) format—or, more simply, e-mail enhanced with graphics. Today, approximately 60 percent of e-mail users have the ability to receive these more visual e-mails. According to Jupiter Research, HTML gets a 200 percent better response than plain text. The catch-22: Some people choose to block HTML-formatted e-mails.

CA$HVERTISING Tip: Do an A-B Split. Compare the response you get from HTML versus text-only promo. Chop your list in half and mail each version at the same time. The increased response power of a well-constructed HTML e-mail may out-pull a text-only e-mail with higher deliverability.

4. Best Way to Get Your E-Mails Opened

According to *Opt-In News*, 69 percent is the average "open rate" for opt-in, business-to-business ezines; 60 percent or higher is considered excellent. What affects your "open rate" most?

1. Familiar sender (use your name if they'll recognize it).
2. Personal subject line (always include your recipient's name).
3. Offer of interest (precision-target your market).

5. Ad Size and Readership

As is the case with print advertising, in online advertising, "skyscrapers" (vertically tall ads) and "leaderboards" (large banners) are more effective than regular-sized banners. In addition, large ads are more effective than small, and interactive (DHTML) ads are more effective than non-interactive. These findings resulted from a study performed for C-NET, and they confirm that human beings do *not* act dramatically different online or off, as print advertising research shows similar patterns of response. So much for today's techies who keep parroting the inaccurate line, "The rules for online advertising are different!" As with all other forms of advertising, an online banner ad will either do well or poorly depending how well it adheres to the foundational, immutable principles of advertising, such as those featured in this book.

6. Animation Click-Through Booster

Animated ads generate click-through rates at least 15 percent higher than static, motionless ads, and in some cases as much as 40 percent higher. Why? Movement catches attention. It's part of a survival mechanism that alerts us to oncoming danger. But does this mean your ads should be littered with movement for the sake of movement? No. Test simple moving elements that enhance your sales message.

Caution: Rapidly flashing elements are annoying. The goal is to *attract*, not irritate. Consider transitions, wipes, fades, and other similar actions.

7. Mystery Ads Score High Click-Throughs

...but low conversion to sales. Cryptic online ads and e-mails can increase click-through by 18 percent, says one study. The problem? Lots of clicks, few sales. Why? Poor targeting. Send your mortgage solicitation to names in the phone book. Write on the envelope in big letters: "SEX!" Most people *will* open the envelope. Even those who don't need a mortgage. But you can't blame them, can you? Sex and survival are the Life-Force 8 granddaddies of them all. The problem is, "SEX!" made them open the envelope, not your wonderful low-interest adjustable. So next time try: "Need a Low-Interest Mortgage?" You're then using the right words on the right audience. Fewer will open your e-mail, but those who do will be better prospects.

Remember: Don't confuse clicks for sales.

Ad-Agency Secret #32:
Multi-page Your Way to Success

Ad agency media buyers understand the importance of repetition. They know that every time their commercial runs, they likely have only a fraction of your attention. So they run it repeatedly in hopes of making their point. If it didn't affect you the first 10 times you saw it, they hope the next 50 showings will compel you to buy.

The same strategy applies to print advertising. You can't just place one ad once and be done with it. Just the same as that TV commercial, your first ad might not catch your prospects' attention. Only a certain percentage will read any individual insertion. That's the importance of *frequency*. Extensive testing by Starch Research has shown that placing more than one ad in the same issue of the same publication can be remarkably effective, and have a 1 + 1 = 3 effect that no single ad can replicate. If you want to make some waves in your market, here are 10 ways to do it.

The 10 Most Effective Multi-ad Formations

1. Three single-page ads in sequence on the right side.
2. Two-single page ads in different sections of the same issue on the right side.
3. Double-page spread.
4. Single-page ads on the right.
5. Single-page ads on the left with strip ad on the right.
6. Single-page ads on the left.
7. Right-page checkerboard (one quarter-page ad in each of the page's four corners).
8. Left-page checkerboard ads.
9. Half-page ad, upper right.
10. Half-page ad, lower right.

Ad-Agency Secret #33: Guarantees That *Guarantee* Higher Response

Do you believe in your product or service? How strongly? I offer a full one-year money-back guarantee on many of my products. Why? It instills confidence in buyers and puts them at ease. They think, "Drew must feel pretty confident about this product. I have a full year to re-turn it and get all my money back. How can I lose?"

Buyers feel vulnerable. In exchange for their hard-earned money, they take a leap of faith every time they give some of it away. They won-der if what they're buying will be worth at least the value of the money they've exchanged for it. And between the time they release their legal tender and the time they experience the product, there's a period of stress and uncertainty. The higher the dollar amount of the transac-tion, of course, the greater the stress. Buy a rotten apple, and it won't ruin your day. But buy a house and find out five years later that the title was forged and you never really owned it, and say hello to an "Excedrin headache" that'll span six seasons.

During the Great Depression, people were extremely cautious about spending what little money they had. Counter to the logic of the times, Hormel ran a large ad in a Chicago newspaper featuring an illustration of an apron-clad grocer holding a can of soup in his outstretched hand. Here's how it began:

DOUBLE YOUR MONEY BACK

...if you don't say this NEW Home-Style Vegetable Soup is the most delicious you ever bought.

THE OFFER Friday and Saturday only. Go to your nearest food store. Pay the regular price of 13¢ for one big 20 oz. container of Hormel Flavor-Sealed Vegetable Soup, following instructions on the label. If you don't agree that it's the best vegetable soup you ever bought, return the empty container to your grocer...who is authorized to pay you back TWICE what you paid.

It was the first time an advertiser had the courage to offer a "double-your-money-back" guarantee. Many fearful company execs warned, "Don't do it! With the state of the economy, people are going to buy armloads of soup and return them all for a big profit!"

The ad was a smashing success, and only 12 women took advantage of the guarantee. But the question is: Did the guarantee help close the sale? You better believe it did. It reduced buyers' pre-purchase stress. And most importantly, it gave them the confidence to buy.

Every time your prospect thinks about buying, her head becomes a battleground for two opposing forces: *skepticism* and the *desire to believe*. Now, imagine an old apothecary scale with *skepticism* on one side and the *desire to believe* on the other. Let's say her level of skepticism is a 7 on a scale from 1 to 10, 10 being "most skeptical." And her *desire to believe* is a 5. It's up to you to throw more weight onto the *desire to believe* side in order to offset the amount of skepticism she now experiences. Including a strong guarantee helps lighten the skepticism side and press down on that desire side. Sometimes it's all you need to clinch the sale.

Not only do longer, stronger guarantees boost your sales, but they (ironically) also result in fewer returns. Why? Studies show that short-term guarantees (30, 60, or 90 days) keep customers poised to make the return and force them to be more conscious of the return deadline. Longer guarantees (six months, one, five, 10 years, lifetime) give prospects confidence in the product and avoid the "beat the clock" mindset of using the product and sending it back within the short allotted time.

CA$HVERTISING Tip: Offer the *longest, strongest* guarantee in your industry. (Your competition will hate you for this.) Such a guarantee conveys your confidence in what you sell, which in turn gives prospects the confidence to give you their money. As a bonus, it causes potential buyers to question your competitors' weak—or absent!—guarantee. It also lets you ask—in big bold type—"Why Do Our Competitors Guarantee their [PRODUCT TYPE] for Only 90 Days?" Followed up with the insidious, "Do they know something about their [PRODUCT] that they're not telling you?"

A well-crafted guarantee isn't an afterthought. It's a damned powerful sales tool—one of your most important, especially if your competitors' guarantee is weak by comparison. Show off your guarantee, don't hide it! Surround it with a fancy certificate border and print your signature under it. Include it in your ads, on brochures, your Website, everywhere. Be proud of it! And watch it perform wonders for you.

Ad-Agency Secret #34:
The Psychology of Size

Fact: Bigger ads attract more attention. This idea has been tested by various researchers using different methodologies, and they've all come to this same conclusion. What *hasn't* been quantified, however, is just how much of a proportional increase in attention a larger ad will consistently deliver. Research has shown this: *the attention value of ads is not in direct proportion to its increased size.* In other words, increasing the size of your ad four times will not, in general, multiply the number of readers by four.

So if your boss, client, partner, or spouse says, "Hey, we got 100 replies to our quarter-page ad. Blow it up to a full-page ad so we'll get 400 replies," you need to sit him or her down and have a little talk.

In the following table, the *attention value* of a quarter-page ad is represented as 100 percent. Likewise, the attention value of both the half- and full-page ads are calculated as a ratio to the value of the quarter-page ad.

Okay, let's make this easy. In applied psychologist Walter Dill Scott's experiment (first column, bold type), he had subjects read magazines at their own pace and later asked, "What ads do you remember?" Note that the half-page ad (which was two times the area of the quarter-page) scored 300 percent, or *three times* the attention. The full-page ad (which was four times the area of the quarter page) scored 666 percent, or more than six times the attention. Scott's conclusion: *Attention value exceeds increase of ad size.* This would mean you could double your ad size and get far more than double the attention. Great, right? But wait...

Ratio of Size to Attention	Quarter-Page Control Ad	Half Page (2x size)	Full Page (4x size)
W.D. Scott	100%	300%	666%
E.K. Strong	100%	141%	215%
G.B. Hotchkiss	100%	151%	213%
D. Starch	100%	168%	314%
H.F. Adams	100%	178%	No Data
Averages	100%	187.6%	352%

Stanford University researcher E.K. Strong (creator of *The Strong Interest Inventory*, used today to help people make career choices) believed that using real magazines would skew the test results. "Hey guys, it's not just ad *size* that's influencing your subjects...it's the *ads* themselves!" So Strong created a *dummy* magazine—a mock-up—for his experiment. The results showed that the attention value for the larger ads did *not* increase as dramatically as in Scott's experiment. Strong's Conclusion: *Attention value lags behind increase of ad size.*

New York University Professor G.B. Hotchkiss's study had similar results. Without mentioning anything about the ads themselves, he instructed students in his class to read an article in a magazine, and later asked them to recall what ads they saw.

How about our buddy Daniel Starch? In his classic *Analysis of Over Three Million Coupons* published in 1927, he collected 1,400,000 replies from 907 different ads from various advertisers. This mind-bogglingly extensive study produced results not unlike those of Strong, Hotchkiss, and Adams. Look at the Starch data and you'll see that a half-page scores 68 percent better than a quarter-page and a full-page slightly more than 300 percent better than the quarter.

Starch's conclusion: *Attention value lags behind increase of ad size.* Starch said, "Advertisements brought replies very nearly in proportion to their size, although the smaller sizes had a slight advantage. This may have been due to the possibility that the smaller advertisements...placed more emphasis on securing responses."

University of Michigan psychology professor Henry Adams didn't like *anyone's* studies. He wanted to eliminate every possible variable that didn't directly concern size and attention. *Magazines?* Gone! *Articles?* Removed! *Pictures?* Eliminated! Instead, Adams whipped out his scissors and pasted up colored squares in four different sizes: one inch, one and a half, two, and three square inches. Talk about minimalism. Using a tachistoscope—a short-exposure projection device used to help train WWII fighter pilots to identify enemy aircraft—he exposed his subjects to the material four squares at a time. Long story short: His results were similar to all the others.

So how can we make sense of all this crazy research in a way that's practical for us as advertisers? It boils down to this: *an ad's attention value is approximately proportionate to the square root of the area.* Huh? Okay, this means that if you want to double the attention your ad's now getting, you need to enlarge it 400 percent. (So if it's a quarter-page ad, you need to run a full-pager.) To triple the attention, blow it up 900 percent (which is practical only if you're starting out with a very small ad such as a classified display). You'd otherwise have to go to a multi-page ad, as described in Ad Agency Secret #32: Multi-Page Your Way to Success.

So now you have a rule of thumb that tells you how to boost the number of eyeballs that roll across your ads. Start with a proven-effective ad and more attention = more reading = more convincing = more buying = more dollars in your pocket. Now that's the kind of equation I like!

Ad-Agency Secret #35: The Psychology of Page and Section Positioning

Left page? Right page? Top? Middle? Bottom? Ask 100 different advertisers and you'll get 100 different reasons why your ad should appear in a certain location within a publication. However, few, if any, will have any research to back up their recommendations, but boy oh boy, do they adamantly *believe* it!

Multiple studies of hundreds of issues of magazines and scores of ads in dozens of industries have shown virtually *no difference* in the effectiveness of ads appearing on the inside pages toward the front, middle, or back of any issue, or whether they appeared on left- or right-hand pages. Researchers Starch, Stanton, Nixon, National Magazine, Lucas, and others, generally concluded that what matters most is the ad itself: the strength of its offer, and the execution of the copy and design.

> A good ad will get noticed irrespective of its position within the newspaper.*
>
> —Roper Starch Worldwide
>
> *But four of them get noticed **more**. See "Ad-Agency Secret #36: The Fantastic Four."

Ad-Agency Secret #36: The Fantastic Four

Although there are no clear winners of the left-page vs. right-page debate, as we just discussed, researchers at Starch INRA Hooper uncovered distinct ad-position advantages that are actually worth paying more for. They compared 618 magazine ads occupying cover positions to 10,789 single-page, four-color ads appearing on inside pages. They checked both men's and women's publications, business and consumer, and the findings were consistent. This "Fantastic Four" can help your message stand out in even the most crowded publications. Here are the results:

* Ads appearing on the inside front cover have the highest average "Noted" (seen and recalled) scores with the greatest increase—29 percent—over similar ads run anywhere else in the same issue.

* Ads placed opposite a table of contents earn up to 25 percent higher scores.

* Ads appearing on the back cover score 22 percent higher than ads inside.

* Ads placed on the inside back cover score a 6 percent advantage over inside pages.

So stop fretting about where *inside* the publication your ad runs. That's likely not to make a shred of difference, unless, of course, you choose to fork over more green stuff for the research-proven, higher-attention cover slots.

Ad-Agency Secret #37: Consumer Color Preferences and How Color Affects Readership

Do you know what colors people like most? Dozens of experiments have been made by various researchers in the United States and abroad on the question of consumer color preferences. And as human psychology would have it, the results are pretty uniform across the board. Here, in a nutshell, are the compiled rankings.

Ranking	Color
1	Blue
2	Red
3	Green
4	Violet
5	Orange
6	Yellow

The number-one preference for most people tested is blue, with red a close second, then green, violet, orange, and yellow, ranked exactly in that order. Look at your current sales materials—online and off—and see if they reflect these worldwide findings.

Unfortunately, not all graphic designers are aware of this research (they should be), so it's up to *you* to specify the colors you'd like most prominently featured.

Battles of the Oranges

Men and women differ only slightly in color preferences. Based on 21,000 reports, the order of preference was the same for both men and women, except that men put orange in fifth place and yellow in sixth, whereas women put yellow in fifth place and orange in sixth.

Color Preferences Change With Age

Infants select red as their first choice. Next come yellow, green, and blue. At about 12 to 14 months this preference changes. Red remains in

175

first, yellow second, but blue leaps ahead of green. By the time children are 5 years of age, red, green, and blue are about equal in preference, but yellow is farther down the scale (less appealing). It's during the grade-school years that blue gradually overtakes yellow. This preference direction continues through adulthood. While blue goes up in preference, yellow goes down, and continues to do so through as the individual ages. Preference for red, however remains high.

The Older, the Bluer

Why is blue preferred as we grow older? The universal preference for it may have some connection with what takes place inside the aging human eye. Look inside an old man's (or woman's) eye, and you'll see that the optical lens has hazed, or yellowed. In fact, the lens of the child's eye may absorb only 10 percent of the blue light, whereas an elderly eye may absorb 85 percent of blue light. One theory is that this is nature's way of protecting the eye against painfully bright light as we age.

Most-Loved Color Combos

How much money is spent on multi-color ads every year? Billions. But are some color combinations actually preferred by more people than others? Let's take a look…

According to artists, the primary colors are red, yellow, and blue. Many insist that the best color combinations are those that do not "cross a primary." Unlike artists, psychologists believe there are actually four primary colors: red, green, yellow, and blue. They insist that the best color combinations are those that employ complementary colors. Little experimentation has been done, so the jury is still out, but the studies that *have* been done do show similarities in results.

In one experiment by our ol' researcher buddy Daniel Starch, 32 men and 25 women (with 25 artists as observers/judges) were shown paired colors to determine which combinations they preferred. The results were conclusive. Consumers preferred colors of low *Value* (lightness or darkness) and high **Chroma** or *Saturation* (purity of color). Those combinations consisting of large areas of blue were ranked high. Those consisting large areas of orange and yellow were ranked low:

Consumer Preference	Color Combination
1 (Most liked)	Blue and Yellow
2	Blue and Red
3	Red and Green
4	Purple and Orange
5 (Least liked)	Red and Orange

Bottom line? It m akes good sense to use the higher-ranked color combinations in your next ad, brochure, flyer, email, or website. You'd be tapping into documented research, rather than simply letting your designer choose what colors he or she likes best.

Most Effective Paper and Ink Combos

Readership studies confirm that white and yellow are the two best paper colors for easy reading. Use black, dark blue, and red inks for maximum impact. The best combination? Black ink on yellow paper. Worst? Red ink on green paper, an optically repulsive mix that's practically unreadable—completely unreadable if you're colorblind!

Colorful Research

Starch Research shows that color not only attracts readers, but also gets them more involved. What's more, color also encourages more in-depth reading by:

* ❋ 60 percent over black-and-white only ads.
* ❋ 40 percent over two-color only ads.

In fact, color does more to affect whether your ad gets seen than does size. So if it costs less to add color than it does to run a larger ad, opt for color. In fact, research says that there's a bigger difference in readership between a black-and-white and a four-color ad than there is between a one- and two-page color ad!

> Black & white ads work best when emphasizing end benefits, demonstrating dramatic situations and appealing to the intellect.
>
> —Starch Research

Ad-Agency Secret #38:
The Psychology of Pricing

What's the difference between $19.98 and $20.00? No, I don't mean two cents. (I can figure *that* out myself.) I mean, psychologically, motivationally, persuasively?

It's *psychological pricing*, and you see it used everywhere from department stores to restaurants to furniture retailers, even jewelers. Wal-Mart is known for its heavy use of psychological pricing, with their favorite end digits being "97."

Odd-even pricing theory says that prices ending in odd amounts such as 77, 95, and 99 suggest greater value than prices rounded up to the next whole dollar. $9.77 seems like a better deal than $10.00. And 64 cents for a pound of bananas seems to be an okay price...but 70 cents? You gotta be kidding! But it's more than the idea of saving a few cents. For advertisers like you and me, the effects of such a seemingly simple technique can be dramatic.

Prestige pricing, by contrast, says that if you want something to be perceived as higher quality, you use only *rounded* whole numbers when pricing. For example, $1,000.00 suggests higher quality than $999.95, simply because we've been conditioned to interpret *fractional pricing* as suggestive of value. Upscale retailer Nordstrom department store uses prestige pricing, and so do many fine jewelers and other sellers of high-end merchandise. Surf over to SaksFifthAvenue.com and you'll see only 00s. In fact, the only *cents* you'll see are in the prices of the few featured sale items.

Fractional pricing is more widespread than you probably realize. Researchers Holdershaw, Gendall, and Garland (1997) found that approximately 60 percent of advertised retail prices ended in 9, 30 percent ended in 5, 7 percent ended in 0, and the remaining seven digits, combined, accounted for just more than 3 percent of the prices studied.

But why does this work? Psychologists say that (1) *fractional pricing* suggests that the seller has calculated the lowest possible price, thus the odd number, and (2) we ignore the last digits rather than mentally rounding up. *Doing so allows us to justify a purchase that may be teetering on the threshold of affordability.*

Schindler and Kibarian (1996) tested odd pricing using three versions of a direct-mail women's clothing catalog. All three catalogs were identical, except for the prices, which ended in 00, 88, and 99. The winner? The 99 catalog produced 8 percent greater sales and more buyers than the 00 version. The 88 catalog pulled in as many sales and buyers as the 00 version.

In 2000, Rutgers University did a study of people reading an ad for a woman's dress. The subjects reported that the dress priced at $49.99 was of lower quality than the same ad featuring the *exact same* dress priced at an even $50.

Interestingly enough, people make some fascinating rationalizations for fractional prices. For example, Schindler (1984) found that consumers who see a price ending in 98 or 99 are more likely to believe that the price was not recently raised. (How anyone jumps to that conclusion I'll never understand.)

According to Quigley and Notarantonio (1992), subjects who saw an ad with a 98 or 99 ending price were much more likely to believe the product was on sale than products with 00 end prices.

What about prices ending in 95? Are they as effective as 99? Research shows they're not. Likewise, 49, 50, and 90 are also not suggestive of low price. But evidence shows that prices ending in 79, 88, and 98 do convey value.

Psychological pricing isn't a random game of picking numbers out of a hat, it's a well-researched topic with great implications for your bottom line. And now that you've read what consumers think and what research recommends, how do *your* prices look now?

Ad-Agency Secret #39:
The Psychology of Color

Paint a prison's walls pink, and there's less inmate violence. Put a baby in a yellow room, and the crying begins. Want to suppress your appetite? Try the "Blue Wall Diet Plan." Likewise, red classrooms hype kids up, blue rooms chill them out. Volunteer fundraisers who wear pink uniforms get bigger donations, and sage-green hospital corridors ease patients' frazzled nerves.

Color affects us strongly, including our perception of *weight*. For example, lifting and carrying boxes all day long can be a real drag. So to give its employees some relief, a manufacturer painted their heavy-looking black boxes light green. Voila! Psychologically "lighter" boxes. To make its packaging look heavier, a food manufacturer changed to a darker-colored package. Voila! "More" food inside.

Don't confuse this phenomenon with fashion experts' advice to wear black for its "slimming" effect. Because of its ability to hide shadows caused by "beer and brownie bulges," black clothing helps smooth the body's contours. This in turn causes less attention to be paid to individual "problem areas" by presenting the body's outline as a single optical unit without specific points of interest. That's why bodybuilders look beefier in white and light-colored shirts. All those shadows—readily contrasted against the light-colored cloth—add depth to their musculature.

This "darker is heavier" illusion is called *apparent weight*. And it's simply a matter of choosing the right color to give you the *weight perception* you're looking for.

In an article in the *American Journal of Psychology* entitled "The Effect of Color on Apparent Size and Weight," psychologists Warden and Flynn ran some tests. They put eight boxes—all the same size—in a glass display case. They had people randomly look at each box, in varying order, and asked them to rank the boxes according to how much they thought they weighed. Here are the results, from lightest to heaviest:

Box Color	Scoring (Higher="Heavier")
White	3.1
Yellow	3.5
Green	4.1
Blue	4.7
Purple	4.8
Gray	4.8
Red	4.9
Black	5.8

Color can even affect taste. Dr Pepper Snapple Group's Barrelhead Sugar-Free Root Beer was advertised as full-bodied, draught-style root beer. When packaging experts Berni Corp. changed the background color on the cans of their sugar-free beverage to beige from blue, people reported that it tasted more like good-old-fashioned frosty-mug root beer, even though the recipe never changed. Similarly, consumers say that darker-colored orange drinks taste sweeter.

Colors—if strongly associated with other products—can also confuse. In the beverage industry, for example, Coca-Cola "owns" the color red. When Berni Corp. designers changed Canada Dry's sugar-free ginger ale can from red to green and white, sales shot up more than 25 percent. The red can had made consumers think "cola."

Because of its power to not only draw attention, but also *alter perception* in ways that even the experts can't explain, ad agencies are hypersensitive to how they use color in their ads and packaging. And now that we know these facts, you and I should be too.

> Results from a study of 21 languages revealed that words for basic colors enter language almost universally in the following order: 1. Black and white. 2. Red. 3. Green or yellow. 4. Yellow or green. 5. Blue. 6. Brown. 7. Gray, purple, pink, and orange.
>
> —Berlin and Kay (1969)

Ad-Agency Secret #40:
Wrap Your Ads in White

It's quick, easy, takes no time or skill, and research shows *it works*. It's the power of *white-wrap isolation*. It's another one of those little-known and little-used agency secrets revealed by decades-old testing that can give your ad response a lift.

Buy more ad space—say a half-page instead of a quarter—but instead of filling it with more copy and pictures, put your original quarter-page ad smack in the center of it, wrapping your ad with white space. Multiple experiments by researchers Poffenberger and Strong conclude that, for example, a white-wrapped quarter-page ad will get more attention than a fully fleshed-out half-page ad loaded with text and graphics. Poffenberger's tests showed the following improvements due to white-wrapping:

The Attention Increase of White-Wrap Isolation

Standard Composition	White-Wrapped
Half-Page = 100%	**Half-Page = 176%**
Full-Page = 141%	N/A

Strong advises that the additional space purchased should not exceed 60 percent of the area of the advertisement itself. According to Strong, "If more than 60 percent is used, the increased cost will not be compensated by a corresponding increase in attention value. Furthermore, about 20 percent additional used as white space about the advertisement gives the greatest increase in effectiveness, cost considered."

Ad-Agency Secret #41:
Give Yourself a "Cleverectomy"

It's frustrating. Trying to create effective advertising for people who don't know the first thing about it—but *think* they do—is enough to make you rip your hair out of your skull.

A Zen master once said that the best way to learn anything is to first empty your head of preconceptions to make room for new knowledge.

For example, I invite you to listen in on a conversation I had with a Web designer about a headline I wrote for him. It's the most colorful way I know to teach you this lesson.

Scott: This headline stinks! "Powerful Web Pages Designed in 24 Hours by Famous Marketing Expert for $199" isn't very creative!

Drew: Agreed. Not at all.

Scott: Well, can't we do a little play on words, a pun, or give it a twist?

Drew: Why give it a twist?

Scott: To make it catchier. You know, so more people read it. Something like, "Only $250 Keeps You from Getting Caught in a Sticky Web on the Net."

Drew: [Suppressing a laugh] The purpose of your headline is not to be "catchy," Scott. It's to be effective. Being creative for the sake of being creative is a waste of time and money, and is a complete misunderstanding of the principles of creating a headline. Allowing yourself to be seduced by the thrill of creating a "clever" headline that will impress friends and family (but not your prospects) is a terrible mistake! Besides, that "Sticky Web" headline is ridiculous! It doesn't tell the reader what you're selling! And because 60 percent of people who read ads read only the headlines—they scan—you'll lose at least 60 percent of your audience. I teach these ideas in my small-business audio seminar.

Scott: I disagree. Major corporations create very catchy headlines and win awards for them all the time. Did you ever see the commercials during the Super Bowls? Very creative stuff.

Drew: [Sigh] You're right. They *do* win awards. And the Super Bowl commercials are very creative indeed. But "creative" does not mean "effective." If you can develop a headline that contains all the elements of one that could be a potential winner, why would you want to junk it up by trying to be clever?

Scott: Why not make it clever first, and then make it effective—that way you accomplish both things. The "Sticky Web" headline can get people curious to read more.

Drew: But what happens to those who don't get curious enough and don't read any further than that headline?

Scott: They weren't prospects.

Drew: Not true! They may have very well been prospects, but because they had *no clue* what you're selling, they didn't bother to read any further. You outright lost them!

Scott: Yeah, well...

Drew: Well nothing! Advertising is *not* supposed to be entertainment! You may be entertained by it, but that's not its purpose. It's not a creativity contest. It's not meant to grace the walls of the Louvre in Paris. It's also not poetry, comedy, or a riddle to be figured out. Advertising is not about winning awards for being tricky, off-the-wall, or ingenious. Advertising—plain and simple—is about selling products and services. It's business communication with the goal to increase sales by interesting people enough in a product or service that they ultimately trade their money for it.

Scott: But that doesn't mean it has to be boring!

Drew: Did I say anything about boring? It should always be interesting! But something doesn't have to be clever or tricky to grab and hold a prospect's attention. You don't write copy to appeal to the masses that aren't buyers for your product as a way to thank them for reading your ad! And those who are interested in the offer don't need entertainment in order to buy. They need benefits. Facts. An offer. And reassurance that you'll deliver what you promise.

Scott: I still feel that we can do something more than simply state what we're selling.

Drew: Read it again, Scott. This headline does much more than just state what you're selling. It has punch; it capitalizes on people's need for instant gratification by saying you'll deliver in 24 hours; it capitalizes on your credibility as an expert by outright stating you are one; it appeals to those looking to save money; it's specific; it makes an offer; it's clear; it doesn't ask the reader to figure out what it means; and it gets your point across quickly. Who do you think it will appeal to?

Scott: [Silence]

Drew: It will appeal to those who need a Web page, want it done by a pro, need it created quickly, and don't want to spend a fortune. *Your market!*

Scott: Well, I guess we can try it.

Drew: Exactly. Try it. Advertising must be tested to be sure. And because you like the "Sticky Web" concept so much, maybe you want to sink a few thousand dollars on it and see if you get any response from the few people who will read past the headline.

Scott: Very funny.

Drew: Was I laughing?

Bottom line: In advertising, it's not clever to be clever.

Let's say you have $1,000,000 tied up in your little company and suddenly your advertising isn't working and sales are going down. And everything depends on it. Your future depends on it, your family's future depends on it, other people's families depend on it. Now, what do you want from me? Fine writing? Or do you want to see the goddamned sales curve stop moving down and start moving up?

—Rosser Reeves, CEO, Ted Bates Advertising Agency, creator of the "Unique Selling Proposition" (USP) concept

CHAPTER 4

Hot Lists: 101 Easy Ways to Boost Your Ad Response

22 Response Superchargers

1. **FORGET** style—*sell* instead!
2. **SCREAM** "Free Information!"
3. **WRITE** short sentences and keep them reading.
4. **USE** short, simple words.
5. **WRITE** long copy.
6. **BOIL** it down; cut out the fluff!
7. **STIR** up desire by piling on the benefits.
8. **SHOW** what you're selling—action shots are best.
9. **GET** personal! Say: *you, you, you.*
10. **USE** *selling* subheads to break up long copy.
11. **PUT** selling captions under your photos.
12. **WRITE** powerful visual adjectives to create mental movies.
13. **SELL** *your* product, not your competitor's.
14. **DON'T** hold back, give them the *full* sell now!
15. **ALWAYS** include testimonials!
16. **MAKE** it ridiculously easy to act.
17. **INCLUDE** a response coupon to encourage action.
18. **SET** a deadline to break inertia.
19. **OFFER** a free gift for quick replies.

20. **SAY** the words *Order Now!*
21. **OFFER** free shipping.
22. **BOOST** response 50 percent or more with a "Bill Me" or credit option.

9 Ways to Convey Value

1. **SCREAM** "Sale!"
2. **GIVE** them a coupon.
3. **DIMINISH** the price: "Less than a cup of coffee a day."
4. **EXPLAIN** why the price is low: "Our boss ordered too many!"
5. **AMORTIZE** it: "Just $1.25 a day."
6. **BOOST** the value: Tell what it's worth, not only what it costs.
7. **TELL** how much others have paid (and were happy to do so!).
8. **CREATE** a sense of scarcity with deadlines.
9. **EMPLOY** psychological pricing.

13 Ways to Make Buying Easy

1. **GIVE** your street, e-mail, and Web address.
2. **GIVE** your phone number.
3. **PROVIDE** street directions and parking advice.
4. **SAY** "It's Easy to Order..."
5. **ACCEPT** phone orders.
6. **ACCEPT** mail orders.
7. **ACCEPT** online orders.
8. **ACCEPT** fax orders.
9. **ACCEPT** credit cards.
10. **ACCEPT** personal checks.
11. **GET** a toll-free phone number.
12. **INCLUDE** a long, strong guarantee—longer than your competition's.
13. **OFFER** installment payments for products more than $15 ("3 easy payments of just $10.99"), shown to boost response 15 percent.

188

11 Ways to Boost Coupon Returns

1. **TELL** them in the headline or subhead to return the coupon.
2. **SAY** "Buy 1 Get 1 Free!" instead of "50% Off."
3. **USE** a big "FREE!" at the top of your ad.
4. **TELL** what the coupon brings; say it again inside the coupon itself.
5. **SHOW** what the coupon brings with a small photo or illustration.
6. **USE** a bold coupon border.
7. **SET** a *hard* (firm date) or *soft* deadline ("The First 100 People...").
8. **PROVIDE** check-off boxes to get people involved.
9. **SAY** "Valuable Coupon" at the top.
10. **GIVE** sufficient room for fill-ins.
11. **POINT** to the coupon with bold arrows.

46-Point "Killer Ad" Checklist

Here's a fast and easy way to help ensure your ads contain the ingredients for success. Check all that apply to your ad; the more, the better.

Headline

[ ] Does it feature your product's biggest benefit? (The #1 most important rule.)

[ ] Is it a real grabber? Does it elicit an emotional response ?

[ ] Does it use any of the 22 Psychologically Potent Headline Starters shown in Chapter 3?

[ ] Is it significantly larger than your body copy? Boldfaced too?

[ ] Is it powerful enough to get people to read your body copy?

[ ] Does it make some kind of offer?

[ ] Is it authoritative, and not wimpy?

[ ] Is the headline set in initial caps? (This Is Initial Caps.)

189

Use ALL CAPS only if your headline is short—about four to five words or so.

[ ] Is it in quotes? This can boost reading 25 percent.

Body Copy: First Sentence

[ ] Are you using one of the dozen body copy jump-starters shown in Chapter 3?

[ ] Does it naturally flow from the headline?

[ ] Does it get right into the benefits for the reader, instead of bragging about your company?

[ ] Does it almost force them to read the second sentence?

[ ] Is *you* one of the first few words?

Body Copy: General

[ ] Does it focus on how the reader will benefit?

[ ] Does it tell your readers why they should buy from *you*, rather than from a competitor who offers the same product/service?

[ ] If your product or service is exciting, does your ad *sound* exciting?

[ ] Does it progress in a logical, methodical way?

1. Get attention.
2. Stimulate interest.
3. Build desire.
4. Offer proof.
5. Ask for action.

[ ] Are you trying to sell only one product at a time? (This is best. However, some businesses, such as: delicatessens and furniture stores, can get away with more. Those are more similar to catalog ads: "Here's everything we got.")

[ ] Do you use selling subheads to break up long copy blocks to make them easier on the eye?

[ ] Is the copy colorful, sprinkled with power visual adjectives where appropriate?

[ ] Is it believable? (Not overblown or ridiculous.)

[ ] Is it respectful of the reader and not insulting to his or her intelligence?

[ ] Is it emotional? Does it create emotion (positive or negative)?

[ ] Do you use the principle of extreme specificity?

[ ] Are your words, sentences, and paragraphs short? Simple words?

[ ] Are your printed ads, sales letters, brochures, and such set in a serif typeface, such as Schoolbook? Is your Web copy set in a sans-serif typeface such as Arial or Verdana?

[ ] Do you tell your readers what you want them to do in a super-simple way?

   1. Clip this coupon.

   2. Bring it to our store by August 21.

   3. Save 50%.

[ ] Do you outright ask for the sale?

[ ] Did you set a deadline, if appropriate? (Most of the time it is!)

[ ] If you have a lot of benefits to offer, do you list them in bullet or numbered form?

[ ] Do you use testimonials? If you don't have them, get them!

[ ] Is your business name and phone number large and instantly noticeable?

[ ] Did you include your logo? (Use it all the time—the more often people see it, the more brand equity it builds.)

[ ] Do you give directions, maps, or landmarks? (They may be more necessary than you think.)

[ ] Did you key your ad to better track responses?

Layout and Design

[ ] Did a professional designer produce your ad? (Not a layout person!)

[ ] Is your headline big and bold?

[ ] Is the headline broken at the right words? For example:

WRONG WAY:

Now You Can Throw

Away Your Glasses and

Enjoy 20/20 Vision Again!

RIGHT WAY:

Now You Can Throw Away

Your Glasses and Enjoy

20/20 Vision Again!

[ ] Is the ad easy to read? Is there a focus? (The eye should naturally be pulled to certain areas first, not jump around.)

[ ] Is there sufficient white space? Did you wrap it in white?

[ ] Did you indent your paragraphs? This makes reading easier.

[ ] Is the number of separate elements kept to a minimum? (Don't have a million little tint blocks with type, three bursts, two blocks of bullets, a corner flag, and four reverse-type panels!)

[ ] Do you use art (photos or illustrations) relevant to your sales message? (Please, no babies for steel-belted tire ads!)

[ ] Did you use a minimum number of typestyles? (One or two; three max! Unless a professional designer recommends it in a unique situation.)

[ ] Do you feature a picture of a person looking at you? (It's one of the most powerful ways to grab people's attention.)

Epilogue

Whether you realize it or not, you now know more about how to create effective advertising than the majority of your competitors. Want to prove this? Ask them about any of the ideas we've discussed. In response, you'll likely get wrong answers and blank stares. That's because most of your competition is too busy running their businesses to stop and learn how to make them more successful. I congratulate *you* for doing so. In fact, the tips, tricks, techniques, and little-known principles I've shared with you in *CA$HVERTISING* are the same that a marketing consultant or ad agency would use if you hired them for big bucks. There's no reason you can't use them yourself and reap the rewards.

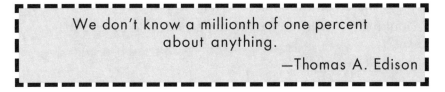

> We don't know a millionth of one percent about anything.
>
> —Thomas A. Edison

My 23 years in the ad business has taught me a lot, but it has only been since WWII that consumer psychology has been recognized as its own field of study. And even though *advertising* psychology experiments were conducted decades prior—with most of the findings still valid today—there's still much more to learn. The study of the human mind is as infinite as the mind itself.

Make no mistake: the *marketplace* will always be the final arbiter of our work. Even our best efforts might crash and burn, despite following all the rules. But armed with the information in this book, you'll greatly increase your chances of success—that is, if you put it to use.

But don't let your learning end with this book! Make a *study* of advertising. Read the classics featured in my recommended reading list. I don't care if you read only one page a day. Keep your motivation high by feeding yourself the great lessons from the masters of advertising. Get this information into your head so you can refine your approach and increase the frequency of your successes. That's how I did it, and you can do the same, or better.

Remember: No matter what you sell or where you sell it, effective advertising is the engine that can keep your business running in good times and bad.

In the mid-first century AD, Roman philosopher Lucius Annaeus Seneca said, "If wisdom were offered me with the provision that I should keep it shut up and refrain from declaring it, I should refuse. There's no delight in owning anything unshared."

I'm grateful for the appreciation you've expressed by reading this book. It's my sincerest hope that what I do benefits you in even the smallest way. Doing so makes my effort worthwhile.

Although I may not know you personally—or perhaps we've met in my CA$HVERTISING workshops or done business together—I want the fact that we've become friends through the printed word to make a difference for you. If I can assist you in any way, please feel free to contact me at Drew@Cashvertising.com. I'd also love to hear how the ideas I've shared in this book have helped you.

Until then, I wish you health, happiness, and prosperity!

Drew Eric Whitman

September 2008

APPENDIX

Recommended Reading

There's no need for you to read hundreds of books on advertising—just the best. That's why I've compiled a list for you, featuring many of the classics. This list represents centuries of advertising experience by many of the industry's greats...and it's all yours for just a few weeks of enjoyable reading. Talk about a shortcut to success! You'll find no fluff, because I've selected books that contain only solid, put-it-to-immediate-use information. So, start by picking the ones that interest you most, and dig in.

On Copywriting, Advertising, and Marketing

My Life in Advertising and Scientific Advertising, by Claude Hopkins
McGraw-Hill (1966)

Here's a classic by the man who started it all. Claude Hopkins is regarded as one of the greatest copywriters of all time. He pioneered the "Reason-Why" style of copywriting (telling people why to buy your product). It's filled with priceless stories, humor, and practical lessons you can apply to your ads immediately. You can find this book *free* online; Google it!

Advertising Ideas, by John Caples
McGraw-Hill (1938)

This is a super collection of old magazine ads. Caples examines each ad and points out what made it so successful. The ads are quite dated, but the lessons are just as valuable today (basic human desires—the Life-Force 8—do not change).

Tested Advertising Methods, by John Caples
Prentice Hall (1998)
> Another excellent Caples book. A must-read.

Making Ads Pay, by John Caples
Dover Publications (1957)
> Ditto.

Ogilvy on Advertising, by David Ogilvy
Vintage (1985)
> What's it like to climb inside the mind of one of advertising's most iconic legends? Reading this book is probably the closest thing to it. You're sure to come out with a dramatically changed view on how the industry works, *and doesn't*. I've quoted him often in this book because his no-bull approach to advertising resonates strongly with everything I've been teaching for the past 28 years.

How to Write a Good Advertisement, by Victor O. Schwab
Wilshire Book Company (1985)
> This neat little book is a super condensation of the key elements necessary to put together an effective ad. It is easy to read, and is all meat. You could read the entire book in under an hour.

Small-Space Advertising for Large and Small Advertising, by Printers Ink
Funk & Wagnalls (1948)
> This great book was put together by the pioneer advertising magazine, *Printers Ink*. It contains a ton of information about writing and designing small-space ads. Similar to the Caples books, it is dated; however, it's important to realize that people have remained pretty much the same throughout the years. It's loaded with practical tips and suggestions.

Breakthrough Advertising, by Eugene M. Schwartz
Boardroom Classics (1984)
> This is one of my all-time favorites by a wizard of direct response. It discusses the psychology of advertising and the stages your product or service goes through in consumers' minds. It talks a great deal about

headlines, examines how to fire up your copy, and contains some of the hardest-hitting direct-response ads I've ever seen.

The Robert Collier Letter Book, by Robert Collier
Prentice Hall Trade (2000)

This is another big favorite of mine. Focusing on sales letter writing, this fascinating book teaches you how to write copy that strikes at the emotional heart of your prospects. It's an absolute goldmine of great examples, regarded as a classic in the advertising industry. Don't miss it!

The 100 Greatest Advertisements, by Julian L. Watkins
Dover Publications (1959)

Just what the title says: one advertising masterpiece after another. Can you spot what made them so great? A fun journey back in time, and a super learning experience!

Words That Sell, by Richard Bayan
McGraw-Hill (2006), Revised and Expanded Edition

Bigger and better than the top-selling original version, it's a virtual advertising writer's thesaurus by a great guy, a gifted (and hilarious) writer. Packed with more than 6,000 high-powered words, phrases, and slogans. Clever category cross-referencing helps jump-start your creative thinking. Whether you're an advertising newbie or an old pro, it's indispensible!

More Words That Sell, by Richard Bayan
McGraw-Hill (2003)

The popular follow-up title that's packed with 3,500 high-powered, idea-generating words, phrases, and slogans, conveniently arranged by category and purpose. Example categories include: Power Words, Sounds, Technology, and Youth Market. Helps you target your approach for specific niches and fine-tune your copy for desired effects using emotional, cerebral, action verbs, and more. A great way to kick-start your copy no matter what you sell.

Positioning: The Battle for Your Mind, by Al Ries and Jack Trout
McGraw-Hill (2000)

An important book that tells you how to structure your business/company in the market so you are perceived to be different and better.

Teaches you how to choose the best product name, how to strategize using the competition's weaknesses, and more.

The Copywriter's Handbook, by Robert W. Bly
Holt Paperbacks (2006)

A classic guide that's invaluable for anyone who writes or approves copy. Bly shows how to write winning headlines and body copy for ads, brochures, sales letters, magazines, newspapers, TV, radio, e-mails, and multimedia presentations. It was even recommended by the legendary David Ogilvy—high praise indeed.

On Creativity

Systematic Approach to Advertising Creativity, by Stephen Baker
McGraw-Hill (1979)

I couldn't put this book down. Tons of examples, tons of tips, tons of fun!

A Whack on the Side of the Head, by Roger von Oech
Business Plus (1998)

If you'd like to be more creative, this (and the next book) is a good start. Informal and filled with fun exercises and illustrations.

A Kick in the Seat of the Pants, by Roger von Oech
Harper Paperbacks (1986)

Ditto.

On Layout and Design

How to Design Effective Store Advertising, by M. L. Rosenblum
National Retail Merchants Association (1961)

This book takes the mystery out of ad design, and tells you the hows and whys. (Might be difficult to locate.)

Looking Good in Print, by Roger C. Parker
Coriolis Group Books (1998)

Invaluable for anyone who wants to learn the basics of graphic design. Jam-packed and super-easy to read and understand. Highly recommended.

Index

About the Author

Most people determine their career path in high school or college, but **Drew Eric Whitman**—a.k.a. "Dr. Direct!™"—couldn't wait to get started. He began creating advertising at age 11 by writing and designing direct-response catalogs of jokes, gags, and novelties. Complete with product illustrations, order forms, and postage charts, he distributed them to his 5th grade classmates by the armful and collected cash orders in equal abundance. Although his teachers did not encourage Drew's entrepreneurial spirit (they would have preferred that he had done his homework rather than sold whoopee cushions), it marked the beginning of an exciting career in the wacky and wonderful world of creative writing and advertising.

Many years later, after extensive experience in face-to-face selling of everything from printing to clothing and jewelry to real estate, a degree in advertising from Temple University started the ball rolling. Today, Drew is an outspoken, humorous, and philosophical advertising trainer and writer. He worked for the direct-response division of the largest ad-agency in Philadelphia. He was also senior direct response copywriter for one of the largest direct-to-the-consumer insurance companies in the world. He created powerfully effective advertising for companies ranging from small retail shops to giant, multi-million dollar corporations. His work has been used by many of the largest and most successful companies and organizations in the United States including American Automobile Association, Advertising Specialty Institute,

American Legion, Amoco, Faber-Castell, Texaco, Day-Timers, and many others.

Drew is co-author of *The $50,000 Business Makeover Marathon* and developer/producer of the nationally acclaimed *CA$HVERTISING* crash-course advertising seminar.

As a resident of sunny southern California, Drew's creative mind is free from the constricting bounds of his former metropolitan life in Philadelphia. When he's not writing, Drew is thinking about what he *should* be writing, or trying to find the best enchiladas and salsa in Southern California with his wonderful wife, Lindsay, amazing son, Chase, and flat-coated retriever, Joey, the sweetest four-pawed beast on planet Earth.

For more information about Drew's training programs
and products, visit him online at:
www.Cashvertising.com.

What Organizations and Participants Are Saying About Drew Eric Whitman's CA$HVERTISING Seminar

Excellent! Tremendous! One of the finest seminars I have ever attended.
—John P. Cataldo, Sr., executive director,
Greater Warminster Area (Pa.) Chamber of Commerce

What a difference your presentation was. It was worth the attendance fee just to see your performance!
—Steve Galyean, executive director,
Galax-Carroll-Grayson (Va.) Chamber of Commerce

After your presentation, I can end my search for the perfect seminar.
—Linda Harvey, executive director,
Butler County (Pa.) Chamber of Commerce

I am beginning to hear from others who did not attend and are asking when we might do a "repeat" since they are being told they missed the seminar of the year!
—Russ Merritt, executive director,
Rocky Mount (VA) Chamber of Commerce

Outstanding presentation. Your humorous, fast-paced style was simply a great bonus.
—Dee Sturgill, Supervisor, Business and Marketing Education,
State of Ohio Department of Education

The information was relevant and the presentation style was excellent. In fact, it had more information than some eight-hour seminars we've had.
—Diane Schwenke, president,
Grand Junction (Colo.) Chamber of Commerce

Thank you, thank you thank you! Your presentation was very entertaining, as well as informative, and I have heard nothing but positive comments from those in attendance.
—Kimberly A. Belinsky, program manager,
Bloomsburg Area (Pa.) Chamber of Commerce

To say he's enthusiastic, high energy, and knowledgeable on the subject of advertising would be putting it mildly. Drew not only met our expectations, but exceeded them.
—Lee R. Luff, CCE, president,
Findlay-Hancock (Ohio) Chamber of Commerce

205

Without a doubt, you were the best keynote speaker we have had at our annual conference.

—Barbara Cunningham, Business and Industry Specialist, University Extension SBDC, Kansas, City, Mo.

Once you have an audience captive, they are never distracted for one second. Two hours seemed like 10 minutes.

—Carole Woodward, President, Lexington Area (N.C.) Chamber of Commerce

When Asked, "What Did You Like Most About the Seminar?" Participants Said:

I gained a tremendous amount of knowledge. Very useful...very powerful!

—Janell M. Bauer, The Resource Center, Inc.

Everything said was a good idea.

—Andy Raggio, Park Western Leasing

The enthusiasm!

—Kathy Sanders, Mesa Moving & Storage

Drew's enthusiasm and presentation of ideas and facts.

—Kay Albright, Illusions of The Heart

All of it was incredibly helpful and insightful. Amazingly, you covered it all. Your personality and delivery made it fun!

—Debra Hesse, Colorado Easter Seal

Sheer volume of immediately usable information.

—Gina McCullough, Butler Memorial Hospital

Interesting, stimulating speaker. Much valuable information given. I started playing with ad copy almost immediately and had fun with it.

—Donna Armistead, Superior School of Dance

Fast-paced—applicable to what I do.

—Kay Weddle, The Framer's Daughter

Right to the point.

—Chet Grochoski, Calumet Machine

Very entertaining. I liked the fast pace and enthusiasm of the speaker. My mind never wandered...stayed right with him. Very lively!

—Melanie B. Ingram, First National Bank of Ferrum

Lots of information in a short amount of time.

—T. Wayne Cundiff, Cundiff Lumber, Inc.

Well presented. Most informative.

—Linda Burger, Collins-McKee Funeral Services

Direct—to the point—holds your attention.

—Charles D. Easter, Martin Jewelry

Great presentation! Love the energy!

—Mary Etta Clemons, Wythe-Grayson Regional Library

Interesting start to stop.

—David B. Imhof, Imhof Supply, Inc.

Specific information. Novel approach. Lots of information.

—Nancy Monday-Yates, The Unicorn

Excellent speaker, not boring.

—Deborah Sizer, WBOB Radio

My mind did not wander as it usually does during seminars!

—Jan Lubinski, Best Western Kings Inn & Franklin Square Inn

Lively presentation. Obviously knowledgeable.

—Jerry D. Johnson, North Pittsburgh Telephone Co.

Advertising is simple if you know what I learned today.

—Karla Korpela, Evert's Motor Sales, Inc.